SOMEONE I

BLUNDER

THE AUTHOR: After graduating from Oxford, Denis Judd took his Ph.D at London University. He is currently Professor of British Imperial and Commonwealth History at the University of North London, and is a Fellow of the Royal Historical Society. Among his publications are _Empire; the British Imperial Experience from 1765 to the Present, Balfour and the British Empire, Radical Joe: A Life of Joseph Chamberlain, The Victorian Empire, Lord Reading, The Boer War, The Crimean War, Palmerston, The British Raj, Jawaharlal Nehru,_ and with Peter Slinn, _The Evolution of the Modern Commonwealth._

Denis Judd lives in north-west London. He is married and has four children and one grandchild. He has written several documentary programmes for BBC Radio, most recently on the Boer War, and has broadcast often on radio and television.

SOMEONE HAS BLUNDERED

Calamities of the British Army in the Victorian Age

DENIS JUDD

THE WINDRUSH PRESS • GLOUCESTERSHIRE

To Geoff and Victoria with warm thanks for many years of friendship and in admiration at what you have both achieved

First published in Great Britain in 1973 by Arthur Barker Ltd
Reprinted in 1999 by The Windrush Press Ltd
Little Window, High Street,
Moreton-in-Marsh
Gloucestershire GL56 0LL
Tel: 01608 652012
Fax: 01608 652125
Email: windrush@ windrushpress.com
Website: www.windrushpress.com
Text Copyright © Denis Judd 1973 and 1999

ISBN 1 900624 38 9

The cover photographs are reproduced by permission of Peter Newark's Military Pictures and show (front): 'Last Stand of the 44th at Gundamuck in the Retreat from Kabul, 1841' painted by W.B.Wollen, 1898; (back): 'The Indian Mutiny 1857-58: Miss Wheeler defending herself against the Sepoys at Cawnpore'

Printed in Malta by Interprint Ltd., Malta

Contents

Preface

This book has grown out of my teaching for the University of London's Optional Subject in Imperial history in which the exploits, and calamities, of Queen Victoria's armies play so important a part. I have set out to examine the reasons for, and the implications of, British military failures in the Victorian age, through an assessment of six significant wars. Though a number of the incidents described in the book are compounded equally of tragedy and farce, there is no intention on my part to mock the bones of those who died so long ago and who tried, however ineffectually, to do their duty.

Denis Judd
LONDON 1973

Preface to paperback edition

I derive great pleasure from the reissuing of this book in a paperback edition. I am equally pleased that it will form part of the excellent Windrush Press list concentrating upon various aspects of military history. The Introduction to the book has been revised in the light of recent research and, indeed, recent military history and developments. The Select Bibliography has been substantially updated, so that the reader may have access to both contemporary accounts as well as to many modern interpretations of the wars that the book analyses.

In the book I have set out to examine the reasons for, and the implications of, British Military disasters and failures during the Victorian Age. Though a number of the episodes described in the book are compounded equally of tragedy and farce, there is no intention on my part to mock the bones of those who died so long ago and who tried, however ineffectually, to do their duty.

Denis Judd
LONDON 1999

Maps and Cartoons

Acknowledgements

The map of the Retreat from Kabul is reproduced from *The First Afghan War* by Lady Sale (Longman); that of Afghanistan and north-west India, by Sidney Blackhurst, from *Signal Catastrophe* by P. Macrory (Hodder and Stoughton); those of the two invasions of Zululand and the Battle of Isandhlwana from *Shaka's Heirs* by John Selby (Allen and Unwin); those of Majuba from *The First Boer War* by Joseph Lehmann (Jonathan Cape); that of the military situation in South Africa from *The Battle of Spion Kop* by Oliver Ransford (John Murray); those of Magersfontein and Stormberg from *Goodbye Dolly Grey* by R. Kruger (New English Library); and those of the Indian Mutiny from *Eyewitness to the Indian Mutiny* editor by James Hewitt (Osprey Publishing). The two cartoons are from the Mary Evans Picture Library.
The author and publishers are grateful to the above for kind permission to reproduce the maps and cartoons.

Introduction:
Soldiers of the Queen

And when we say we've always won,
And when they ask us how it's done,
We'll proudly point to every one
Of England's soldiers of the Queen.
                    (Traditional)

Let us admit it fairly, as a business people should,
We have had no end of a lesson:
    it will do us no end of good.

Not on a single issue, or in one direction or twain,
But conclusively, comprehensively, and several
    times and again,
Were all our most holy illusions knocked higher
    than Gilderoy's kite.
We have had a jolly good lesson,
    and it serves us jolly well right!

Rudyard Kipling, *The Lesson, 1899–1902*

Introduction:
Soldiers of the Queen

The Victorian age is popularly regarded as one of peace and prosperity, when the first industrialized nation, revelling in the new orthodoxy of free trade, aspired to a global commercial supremacy which was guaranteed by both the irresistible flood of its exports and by the guns of the Royal Navy. On this analysis the Pax Brittanica was, in part at least, made in Birmingham and fostered in Whitehall. Between 1815 and 1914 the British Empire went only once to war with a European power – in the Crimea from 1854–6; between 1815 and 1914 Britain remained one of the chief workshops of the world. The equation of peace with prosperity seems, therefore, an obvious one.

In fact the Pax Brittanica rested equally upon the almost ceaseless activities of British arms in an extraordinary variety of colonial wars and punitive expeditions. From 1837 to 1901 there were hardly any years free of fighting of some sort. These conflicts ranged from titanic struggles that threatened the very fabric of Empire (like the Indian Mutiny of 1857–8 and the

Second Boer War of 1899–1902) to little publicized expeditions to obscure regions (like the Bhootan Campaign of 1864–5 or the Waziristan Expedition of 1894–5).

Yet for most of Queen Victoria's reign there was scarcely any attempt to promote a coherent analysis of the problems of imperial defence. Only when British security was challenged by the irruption of parvenu imperialist powers in the last two decades of the century, and by the threatening naval building programmes of foreign states in the 1890's, were there tentative efforts to improve the situation. But the Colonial Defence Committee, founded in 1878 then killed off a year later and revived in 1885 by the Salisbury government, was hardly a distinguished or influential body; nor did the Cabinet Defence Committee, established in 1895, make much impact upon the planning and coordination of imperial defence, since the army and the navy had their own strategic convictions and often sought to keep their own counsels. Queen Victoria had been dead more than a year before Arthur Balfour, the newly appointed Prime Minister, reconstituted the Cabinet Defence Committee in 1902 and transformed it into the far more impressive, though merely advisory, Committee of Imperial Defence.

The cost of defending, and extending, the Empire, and of promoting British interests elsewhere, was shared in three ways between 1837 and 1901 : by the British exchequer, by the government of British India, and by the white-settled self-governing colonies. Of these, the British taxpayer justifiably shouldered the heavier burden : the British regular army numbered about 100,000 in the 1830s and had risen to more than 200,000 by the last decade of the century; the Royal Navy was also financed, for all but the years 1888–1901 of Victoria's reign, solely by the British government.

British India's contribution to imperial defence was, likewise, an enormous one : not only were 70,000 British troops stationed in the sub-continent at India's expense, but there were about 140,000 Indian regulars as well; in this way Indian taxpayers provided the money to pay fellow Indians to uphold the supremacy of the British Raj! But the Indian Army had other uses apart from maintaining domestic law and order; it was employed as an instrument of Imperial policy overseas. In a serious emergency it could also be expanded rapidly – as was shown in 1914–18. Indian troops fought in a number of British wars, from the Crimea in 1854–6 to the Sudan in 1896–9 and the Boxer Rebellion of 1900, thus justifying Lord Salisbury's famous description of India as 'an English barrack in the oriental seas'. There was, however, one serious limitation on the use of Indian troops; they could not easily be employed in South Africa : the Afrikaners of the Transvaal and the Orange Free State were as determined to maintain white supremacy as to resist British domination; thus any attempt to coerce them with non-European troops was a high risk strategy, even though the British eventually took the risk as the Boer War of 1899–1902 dragged on.

The self governing colonies relied heavily upon British protection for a good deal of the Victorian era. But by the early 1870s the cost of local military defence had generally been transferred to their own treasuries, though the South African colonies necessarily proved a partial exception to this trend. In 1887 a further breakthrough came when the Australian colonies and New Zealand agreed to pay an annual subsidy to the upkeep of the Royal Navy, and by 1902 all of the self-governing colonies (apart from Canada) were contributing to naval costs. Even so it remained almost impossible for the British government to pin down the white-settled colonies to any rigid and comprehensive system of military assistance although in the crisis situation of the Boer War of 1899–1902 they mostly rallied spontaneously to the British cause.

Valuable though the Indian Army was, and welcome as colonial contributions were, the British government's responsibility for imperial defence was constant, and sometimes crushing. When in 1897 the Colonial Secretary, Joseph Chamberlain, spoke of Britain as 'the weary titan staggering beneath the too great orb of its fate' he was indulging in a perfectly pardonable exaggeration, for the preceding fifty years had indeed seen the military establishment stagger on several vital occasions and its burdens certainly seemed to be increasing as the century drew to its close.

The fumblings and failings of Victorian military history do not, of course, outweigh the success, since for every Majuba Hill there were any number of Omdurmans and Ulundis. Yet it is the disasters which reveal British military inadequacies in their starkest light.

Between 1815 and the outbreak of the Crimean War in 1854 the regular army was run-down and shamefully neglected. Since the East India Company maintained its own independent army until 1858 the full impact of this military unpreparedness was not felt until the regiments sailed for the Crimea. Parliamentary parsimony had caused the military establishment to be pared to the bone. In 1820 the regular army numbered a mere 80,000, and although by the 1840s the total had crept up to over 100,000 the dispatch of five infantry divisions and one cavalry division to the Black Sea denuded the British and Irish garrisons. More serious still was the unbelievably chaotic state of the army's commissariat and transport arrangements. The hideous confusion that was all too evident in the Crimea is at least partly explained by the fact that army administration was shared between thirteen different departments, many of whose duties overlapped or were at best ill-defined.

The officers and men of early Victorian armies were undeniably brave and, on the whole, stoical. Unfortunately the profession had hardly moved on from the heroic times of the Napoleonic wars. Until 1871 officers could still purchase commissions and promotion up to the rank of lieutenant-colonel; beneath their scarlet jackets the blood of the officer class was often of the noblest blue. They often tended to take their status and their pleasures seriously, their professional duties less seriously. Fox-hunting and gambling were the real pastimes of a gentleman; parade ground drill an onerous bore, as described by an East India Company officer in the early 1850s:

Well, a black rascal makes an oration by my bed every

morning about half an hour before daylight. I wake and
see him salaaming with a cup of hot coffee in his hand.
I sit on a chair ... while he introduces me gradually into
an ambush of pantaloons and wellingtons – if there is a
parade. I am shut up in a red coat, and a glazed lid set
upon my head, and thus, carefully packed, exhibit my
reluctance to do what I am going to do – to wit, my duty
– by riding a couple of hundred yards to the parade.

The rank and file at the time of the Crimean War were mostly
recruited from the dregs of society, grossly underpaid and over-
disciplined. The Duke of Wellington once said of his men 'I
don't know what they do to the enemy, but by God they frighten
me!' Order was maintained, in the last resort by the lash and
a fanatical dedication to routines like the cleaning and polishing
of equipment. The British redcoat was required to obey
instructions like an automaton, and individual initiative was at
a rock bottom premium. Barrack room conditions were often
appalling, and in 1898 Lord Roberts of Kandahar, looking back
over his early Indian service, recalled:

> The men were crowded into small badly-ventilated
> buildings and the sanitary arrangements were as
> deplorable as the state of the water supply. The only
> efficient scavengers were the huge birds of prey called
> adjutants, and so great was the dependence placed upon
> the exertions of these unclean creatures that the young
> cadets were warned that any injury done to them would
> be treated as gross misconduct.

The scandals of the Crimean War inaugurated a period of
steady reform, but the most vigorous attempt to set the military
house in order came with Edward Cardwell's tenure of the War
Office from 1868–74. Between 1855 and 1874, therefore, army
administration was overhauled and conditions of service somewhat
improved. The War Office Act of 1870 exalted the Secretary of
State for War over the Commander-in-Chief and made him

responsible for a substantially unified army. Other significant reforms of the Cardwell era included an attempt to reduce service overseas, short six-year periods of enlistment, and the abolition of the purchase of commissions. A further encouraging development had taken place in 1858 with the establishment of an army Staff College, soon to be based at Camberley.

Valuable as these reforms undoubtedly were, they did not go far enough. No General Staff was created to help keep abreast of the important military changes that were taking place in Germany, the United States and Japan, or to coordinate training tactics and supply throughout the Empire's armies. British governments remained more anxious to limit military expenditure than to improve conditions of service. There was little attempt to relate the army's efficiency to Britain's industrial progress In addition, between 1856 and 1895 the Commander-in-Chief was the royal Duke of Cambridge, Queen Victoria's cousin; he was not only a positive obstacle to many reforms, but also possessed the constitutional right of approaching the Crown direct in military matters.

It is unfortunately not possible to show, therefore, that the post-Cardwell years were dominated by enlightened and progressive officers, wedded indissolubly to their profession and supported by a faultless administrative machine. Nor was the common soldier transformed into a resourceful and guileful campaigner.

The British officer class, despite its unrivalled overseas campaigning experience, continued to appear somewhat amateurish to the more hardened and scientific professionals of European armies and, even during the Great War, the British troops were likened to 'lions being led by donkeys'! The obsession with parade ground drill and an immaculate turn-out hardly abated, and at Laings Nek in 1881 the unfortunate men of the 58th were marched in close order, their regimental colours flying overhead, at the Boer entrenchments. Even the benefits of a Staff College education were no guarantee of success : General Colley had graduated from Camberley with the biggest total of marks on record, yet he went down to a succession of humiliating defeats in the Transvaal campaign of 1880–1; Field-Marshal Wolseley never went to the Staff College, but his fighting career was packed with brilliant triumphs.

The short-service enlisted men were no great improvement on their predecessors bound, until 1847, to their regiments for twenty-one years. Perhaps it was absurd to expect anything else : conditions of service and pay were not improved so dramatically as to lure brisk young men of initiative and drive to the colours; flogging persisted until 1881, the pay was a shilling a day and, whether at home or overseas, service could be a hard and unrewarding slog, as Rudyard Kipling wryly showed in his poem *Tommy*:

> You talk o' better food for us, an' schools, an' fires,
>   an' all :
> We'll wait for extry rations if you treat us rational.
> Don't mess about the cook-room slops, but prove it
>   to our face
> The Widow's Uniform is not the soldier-man's
>   disgrace.
>   For it's Tommy this, an' Tommy that, an'
>   'Chuck him out, the brute!'
>   But its 'Saviour of 'is country' when the guns
>   begin to shoot;
>   An' it's Tommy this, an' Tommy that, an'
>   anything you please;
>   An' Tommy ain't a bloomin' fool – you bet
>   that Tommy sees!

The young short-service soldiers, moreover, were sometimes found to be lacking in stamina when actually on campaign. They could hardly be blamed for their poor physiques and their in-experience, and their superiors must bear the ultimate responsi-bility for their poor marksmanship, but the 'beardless regiments of Aldershot or the Curragh' were nonetheless compared unfavourably with 'the masses of strong men ... who hold India and Egypt'. On the other hand they were outstandingly loyal and reliable, and if, as at Spion Kop in January 1900, they occasionally shirked their duty, it was only after taking fearsome punishment from the enemy.

But even given a thoroughly businesslike and astute commander in charge of battle-hardened veterans, there were still any number of hazards while on campaign. The most obvious problem was that many opponents did not play the game according to the text books or the rules of the Staff college. The unorthodox Boers took every advantage of cover, moved stealthily, and faded away if the going got tough – quite failed to stand up in a fair fight, as Kitchener so bitterly complained. Yet even when the Zulu impis at Isandhlwana predictably ran in a dense mass at their enemies they were still able to triumph through persistence and remarkable courage.

Another difficulty lay in the continuing deficiencies in supply, transport and equipment. Especially when faced with guerillas harrying supply routes, Victorian expeditions deployed an inordinate amount of manpower simply to keep communications open. When, as in Afghanistan, they failed to achieve this, disaster was always imminent; when, as in South Africa between 1899 and 1902, the supplies were kept moving, it was only at the cost of removing an enormous number of troops from frontline fighting duties.

There were other vagaries of supply, some of them extremely petty. At Isandhlwana there was both a lack of screwdrivers and an excess of 'red tape', consequently the ammunition boxes were not opened quickly enough to stave off the impis. At Majuba Hill, General Colley did not possess an accurate map, and thus led his force to an untenable position on the summit. In both the Zulu War and the First Boer War the Martini-Henry rifle kicked like a mule and soon overheated. Until 1881 the bright red jackets of the infantrymen provided ideal targets for enemy sharp-shooters and were at the same time stiflingly hot in the tropics and on the veld.

Despite all this, Victorian Britain's technological expertise, and the hallowed regimental traditions, discipline and endurance of the troops, ought to have been more than a match for Afghans, sepoys and Zulus – even for Boers and, arguably, for Russians too. But even when the meddlings of distant Cabinet ministers and not so distant proconsuls were not particularly obstructive, some singular disasters overtook British arms.

It is, of course, by no means inevitable that a great world power boasting the very latest in military hardware and communications techniques will triumph over apparently 'inferior' opponents, as the twentieth century has so vividly illustrated. After all, the Russian experience in Afghanistan in the 1980s was scarcely less disastrous than that of the British under Queen Victoria; the United States comprehensively lost the war against the Communists in Vietnam; Britain withdrew in despair and frustration from Palestine in 1948, and subsequently found great difficulty in maintaining control over a number of rebellious, though 'backward', colonial possessions from Kenya to Aden; the Anglo-French assault on Egypt during the Suez crisis palpably failed to achieve its objectives, although international pressure was largely responsible for that; even in the 1999 NATO war against Serb aggression in Kosovo, the Serbian forces managed to withdraw with much of their armoured equipment unscathed, mainly through the simple expedient of fooling their militarily sophisticated enemies into attacking dummies of tanks rather than the real thing.

During the Victorian era the failings of individual commanders certainly accounted for some of the setbacks British forces experienced. Lord Elphinstone's poor health and notorious lack of resolve go far to explain the Afghan disaster of 1842; General Wheeler was too cautious, timid even, before the siege of Cawnpore; Lord Chelmsford seems to have strolled almost casually to early defeat in Zululand in 1879; at Majuba Hill it was arguably either General Colley's college based overconfidence or his lack of experience in the field that provided the fatal flaw; at the start of the Boer War in 1899 General Buller's great public reputation camouflaged his fumbling lack of self confidence.

A further explanation of the causes of military disasters has been persuasively advanced since the first edition of this book, most strikingly by Professor Norman Dixon in his book *The Psychology of Military Incompetence*. In essence the argument is that in a significant number of cases the type of person attracted to the armed forces as officer material, particularly to the British Army, and certainly during the years covered by *Someone Has Blundered*, tend to need the strong structures of military routine and discipline as a support system. Reassurance, peace of mind and satisfaction are gained from 'knowing where you are', from parade ground manoeuvres, from the routines of polishing equipment and brass badges, from obeying and carrying out orders, from being part of a well drilled team, and so forth.

In this context, all goes relatively well on campaign for the vulnerable officer – or indeed other ranker – as long as the military situation seems to be under control, or at least not unexpectedly hazardous. If, however, unforced errors, a surprise attack or, indeed, any unpredictable threat develops, a number of those men who, perhaps unconsciously, have joined the forces for the routine security which enables them to cope with stress and pressure simply collapse or make irrational decisions or become unable to act. If the officer affected is high ranking, a commander-in-chief perhaps, the consequences for his men and for the military are disastrous. This thesis can be applied to the Victorian age as confidently as to any other.

Whatever the most convincing explanation, far too often there was a devastating conjunction of unfavourable circumstances – a devil's brew of incompetence, unpreparedness, mistaken and inappropriate tactics, a reckless underestimating of the enemy, a brash overconfidence, a personal or psychological collapse, a difficult terrain, useless maps, raw and panicky recruits, skilful or treacherous opponents, diplomatic hindrance, and bone-headed leadership. The results then, as we shall see, provided some of the darkest and most humiliating chapters in the history of the Victorian army.

Part I
The Invasion of Afghanistan
1838–42

Our gallant fellows in Afghanistan must be reinforced
or *they will all perish*

Colin Mackenzie, 1841

When you're wounded and left on Afghanistan's plains,
An' the women come out to cut up what remains,
Jest roll to your rifle an' blow out your brains
An' go to your Gawd like a soldier.
Go, go, go like a soldier,
So-oldier of the Queen.

Rudyard Kipling

I

On to Kabul!

On 12 January 1842 General Robert Sale, commander of the East India Company's forces at Jalalabad, was gazing intently, with some of his staff, at the road that led from Kabul. As the officers squinted through their telescopes for some sign of the army they knew to be struggling, like some old bear harried by wolves, through the Afghan passes, Colonel Dennie pronounced a prophesy of doom. 'You will see,' he said, 'not a soul will reach here from Kabul except one man, who will tell us the rest are destroyed.'

Next day, 13 January, the prophesy was eerily fulfilled when, in the words of one of the look-outs, Major Henry Havelock:

> One of us espied a single horseman riding towards our walls. As he got nearer, it was distinctly seen that he wore European clothes and was mounted on a travel-hacked yahoo, which he was urging on with all the speed of which it yet remained master. A signal was made to him by someone on the walls, which he answered by waving a

private soldier's forage cap over his head. The Caubul gate was then thrown open and several officers, rushing out, received and recognized in the traveller the first, and it is to be feared the last, fugitive of the ill-fated force at Caubul in Dr Brydon.

The exhausted Brydon was indeed the only survivor to fight his way through to safety, though a handful of prisoners were later recovered. But of the 4,500 fighting men and 12,000 camp followers that had set out from Kabul only seven days before the overwhelming majority had perished in the snow-filled passes. Afghan muskets, Afghan knives and the bitter Afghan winter had done their work. So had Afghan treachery and British incompetence and muddle. Yet when the British invasion had been launched three years before, there had been no reason to suppose that disaster and humiliation were to be the lot of the combined forces of the East India Company and the British Crown.

The British presence in India, beginning with tentative commercial contacts in the early years of the seventeenth century, had blossomed by 1839 into a sub-continent paramountcy fit to rival that of the great Moguls. The Honourable East India Company had extended its territory through treaty and conquest. It had reduced the Portugese and French holdings in India to insignificant and barely tolerated coastal enclaves; it had brought down rajahs and nizams, and broken Bengalis and Marathas. In the process, however, the Company's commercial activities had dwindled and its administrative and military functions had been greatly enlarged. The ever-expanding frontier of British India was by no means the result of the Company's lust for conquest. Rather it reflected the need to ensure that Indian states bordering on British territory were docile, and preferably friendly, neighbours. When this was in doubt, annexation often occurred.

When the young Queen Victoria ascended the throne in 1837, the stage was set for a fresh diplomatic and military initiative in north-west India. Between Delhi and Afghanistan lay the independent provinces of the Punjab, Sind, Baluchistan and Rajputana. For the moment the Sikhs of the Punjab were inclined to cooperate with the East India Company; the other states posed no immediate threat. But beyond the mountains of Afghanistan there loomed a far greater menace, the threatening shadow of Russia.

Russian expansion into Asia had gathered momentum in the first decades of the nineteenth century. The French threat to India, which had evaporated with Nelson's victory of the Nile in 1798, was thus replaced by a Russian threat. Although the military logistics and the political rewards of a Russian invasion of India remained somewhat obscure, the 'Russian scare' remained a constant stock-in-trade for British military planners throughout the nineteenth century. By 1836 Russia had brusquely extended her influence in Persia, and had encouraged the Shah to lay siege to the fortified city of Herat in western Afghanistan. Herat lay in a fertile plain known as the 'Granary of Central Asia'. But it offered more than grain and fodder to its conqueror, for all the great routes to India from the west passed through Herat.

It now seemed as if the 'gateway to India' was about to fall into Persian hands, and hence under Russian control. In London Lord Palmerston, the Foreign Secretary, was determined to counter Russian influence in Persia with more clear-cut British influence in Afghanistan. When Lord Auckland was appointed Governor-General of British India in 1835 he was specifically charged with taking the Afghan situation in hand. Shortly after he took up his new office Auckland dispatched Captain Alexander Burnes to Kabul as his special envoy.

Burnes had risen like a fiery comet through the ranks of the East India Company's armies. In 1828 he had been transferred to the Company's exclusive Political Branch, and he now embarked on his exacting and hazardous task with a brilliant career behind him and a reputation for determined action and a facility with foreign tongues. Moreover he knew Afghanistan well and had already undertaken a delicate diplomatic mission there.

When in September 1837 Burnes once more entered Kabul he was royally received. The Amir, Dost Mahomed, perturbed by Persian activities on his western frontiers and by Sikh aggressions to the east, welcomed the prospect of substantial British financial aid in exchange for excluding Russian influence. But the East India Company had given Burnes little room for manoeuvre, and there was unfortunately no treasure to pour into the lap of Dost Mahomed. The Amir, though still preferring an alliance with Britain, had also received a Russian envoy who had offered financial support to the Afghans in their resistance to Sikh encroachment. The British were unwilling to antagonize Ranjit Singh, the ruler of the Sikh people, and by the middle of 1838 Burnes's mission had demonstrably failed.

Meanwhile the Persians were pounding on the walls of Herat, and if this ancient citadel fell, then Kabul and Kandahar might well submit, and the Russians could advance to the gates of India. The situation was saved by intense British diplomatic pressure on the Shah of Persia, who eventually abandoned the siege of Herat under the threat of war. With the Persian retreat, the Russian menace was correspondingly reduced. An opportunity now existed to reopen negotiations with Dost Mahomed and arrange for the long-term exclusion of Russian influence from Afghanistan. Unfortunately the Governor-General's Council in Calcutta had already decided to overthrow the Amir.

Much of the responsibility for this decision rests with the Chief Secretary to Lord Auckland's administration – the able and persuasive William Hay Macnaghten. It was a decision that was to lead to the catastrophic retreat from Kabul nearly four years later and to the grisly death of Macnaghten himself. The plan at first rested on the assumption that the mighty Ranjit Singh would cooperate in invading Afghanistan and deposing the allegedly unreliable Dost Mahomed. The Amir's vacant place was to be filled by Shah Suja, who had himself been cast from the throne in Kabul during the civil wars that had ended in Dost Mahomed's elevation to power. Both Shah Suja and Ranjit Singh agreed to a joint invasion.

There were, however, serious drawbacks to this plan. For one thing, the Afghans hated the Sikhs and would undoubtedly resist them ferociously. For another, Shah Suja's chance of being permanently restored to his lost throne would probably be damaged irreparably if Sikh forces helped him to victory. Even if, in the end, Ranjit Singh backed out of his commitment to march into Afghanistan, Shah Suja's cause would then need massive British support to succeed.

As a result of these doubts, the East India Company agreed to provide a strong detachment of the Army of Bombay and 9,500 troops from the Army of Bengal to support Shah Suja's bid for power. British officers also recruited some 6,000 infantry, cavalry and artillerymen for the Shah's levies. This force was to march through the still independent province of Sind, cowing the Amirs on the way, and then advance through the difficult Bolan Pass in the Himalayas into Afghanistan; Quetta, then Kandahar, would be entered, and finally Kabul. The Sikhs would give support by advancing from Peshawur through the Khyber Pass.

It was no small matter to assemble the Company's troops and those of Shah Suja and it was finally arranged that the Bengal regiments should enter Afghanistan first, to be followed by the Bombay regiments and Suja's levies. The preparations of the British forces also left much to be desired, especially in the matter of food supplies. The supreme commander, Sir John Keane, and his staff, assumed that the army would chiefly live off the land, though Afghanistan was hardly a country flowing with milk and honey. To supplement this speculative source of supply, the expedition was to drive enough cattle to provide meat for two and a half months and in addition carry thirty days' allowance of grain.

Partly to assist with the food supplies, but mainly to transport the personal baggage of the British officers, a huge number of camp followers, 38,000 in all, accompanied the troops. The officers of early Victorian campaigns took pains to provide for the pleasures of the mess room and for the comforts of the nightly tent. An appeal to the officers to travel light was ignored, and the invasion force sprouted a monstrous and cumbersome tail. Thousands of cooks, grooms, valets and sweepers trudged behind their masters. 30,000 camels struggled over the inhospitable terrain, and were to prove poor and nervous substitutes for mules and ponies in the Afghan passes. So the expedition set out in December 1838, carrying crate-loads of cigars, table wine, plate, glass, bed-linen, 'dressing cases . . . perfumes, Windsor soap and eau-de-Cologne.' Much of this paraphernalia of European civilization was eventually to be looted by marauding Afghans, or lie smashed and buried under the blood-stained snow drifts between Kabul and Gandamak.

But as the Bengal regiments began their march they exulted in the prospect of conquest, loot and glory. Many British officers expected that eventually they would come face to face with Russian troops when 'to contend at the head of sepoys against the European cohorts of the Czar in the regions beyond the Indus was an honour so rare and unexpected, and fraught with so much promise and distinction and advancement, that not a soldier in the whole length and breadth of India could for a moment tolerate the idea of being left behind.'

The expedition's first task was to subdue the Amirs of Sind and to extract twenty-five lakhs of rupees (£250,000) from them in tribute. This was speedily accomplished, and the Bengal regiments of the army were narrowly diverted from a freebooting assault on the Amirs' capital of Hyderabad which reputedly contained treasure worth eight million pounds sterling. It had been Macnaghten who had insisted on the abandonment of these plans, and even though he was supported by the Governor-General, Lord Auckland, he had clashed bitterly with the commander of the Bengal troops Sir Willoughby Cotton.

Fortunately the quarrel was patched up on Macnaghten's initiative, but it was an early indication of future conflict between the expedition's leaders. Still, at least the troops were unencumbered by booty when they crossed the great river Indus and advanced towards the formidable Bolan Pass. As it struggled over the sharp flints and rough stones of the Pass the army's rations provided a painful contrast between the officers' privileges and the harsh lot of the camp followers: the former ate cold meat, game, bread and butter, and various delicacies washed down with wine and rounded off with brandy and cigars; the latter were reduced to eating sheepskins fried in dry blood.

When the army broke out of the Bolan Pass into open country, hunger faced all of the common soldiers, and the commanders were fearful of mutiny. As General Keane came up behind with the detachments from the Army of Bombay, and Shah Suja and his levies, his troops too were desperate for food. The local ruler, the Khan of Khelat, did what he could to provide supplies, and even guarded the lines of communication through the Pass which the British had unbelievably failed to do, but there was little enough to share among so many. Keane therefore decided to push on with all speed to Kandahar which was entered in triumph in April 1839.

The two sections of the Army of the Indus joined up in Kandahar, and camped there for two months waiting for the crops to ripen. It was not altogether a holiday; Kandahar was an overcrowded and insanitary city, and soon dysentery and fever struck among the stroops. For Shah Suja, on the other hand, the interlude provided him with the opportunity to re-establish his authority over the Afghan people. The reaction of the Kandaharis was mixed, for although some came flocking to offer their services to Shah Suja, the majority remained indifferent and aloof. Suja did not put himself out to win his new subjects' good opinions, and remarked to William Macnaghten that the Afghans were 'a pack of dogs one and all.' For their part, Macnaghten and several British officers were forming the opinion that the deposition of Dost Mahomed would be an extremely unpopular act.

Still, there could be no turning back now, and at the end of June 1839 the Army of the Indus struck camp and marched towards Kabul. In their way lay the ancient fortress of Ghuznee, containing six months' supplies and three thousand fighting men. Sir John Keane's intelligence officers, however, assured him that the fortress would yield easily. Keane hastily revised these opinions when he first saw Ghuznee squatting, huge and menacing, in his path. Uncertain as to the best course of action, the British commander was rescued by an Afghan traitor's information that the fortress's Kabul gate was weaker than the others. Accordingly British sappers blew down the gate with nine hundred pounds of gunpowder, and the European light infantry companies charged over the tangled mass of beams and masonry. Hot on their heels came the main assault column led by Brigadier 'Fighting Bob' Sale.

Within an hour it was all over. The flags of the Army of the Indus flew over the ramparts; 1,200 Afghans lay dead, and 1,500 were taken prisoner. The British forces lost 17 killed and 165 wounded. Mercifully the citadel was not sacked; the few women that were found there escaped rape and, on the whole, those Afghans that surrendered were given quarter. A much more terrible fate, and one indicative of the cruelties of Afghan campaigning, had befallen fifty Ghazi warriors on the day before the attack on Ghuznee. The Ghazis were fanatical supporters of Islam who wished to destroy the infidel invaders and their puppet Shah Suja.

The fifty prisoners were taken off on Suja's orders to be executed. A British officer recorded the bloody scene :

> There were forty or fifty men, young and old. Many were dead; others at their last gasp; others with their hands tied behind them awaiting their doom; and the King's executioners and other servants amusing themselves (for actually they were laughing and joking, and seemed to look upon the work as good fun) with hacking and maiming the poor wretches with their long swords and knives.

This was, alas, by no means the last example of ruthless butchery in the Afghan campaign.

The storming of Ghuznee opened the way to Kabul. The reputation of the invading forces now stood sky high, and Dost Mahomed sent his brother, Jubbar Khan, to negotiate. The Amir offered his submission to Suja, but asked to be made Vizir as recompense. Since it was not uncommon for vizirs to plot against their masters and arrange for them to be discreetly strangled, this request was rejected, and instead Dost Mahomed was offered an honourable asylum in the territories of the East India Company. This he angrily rejected, and prepared to resist the advancing British forces.

But there was to be no battle before the gates of Kabul; the fall of Ghuznee had seen to that. Dost Mahomed's supporters deserted him, thankful to save their skins. The Amir beseeched them to stand by him, reminding them that 'You have eaten my salt these thirteen years, grant me one favour in requital for that long period of maintenance and kindness – enable me to die with honour. Stand by the brother of Futteh Khan when he executes one last charge against the cavalry of these Feringhee (English) dogs; in that onset he will fall; then go and make your own terms with Shah Soojah.'

The appeal was in vain, and Dost Mahomed fled beyond the Hindu Kush, and eventually sought refuge at the court of the Amir of Bokhara. This bloodthirsty and unreliable potentate aspired to Dost Mahomed's former power, and soon clapped him into the vile and pestilential dungeons of Bokhara. But within a few months Dost Mahomed had escaped and roused the Afghan tribes between the Hindu Kush and the river Oxus. The British, who had several months before installed Shah Suja in Kabul, tried to hunt him down but failed to defeat him in open battle. At last Dost Mahomed provided the solution to the hiatus by riding to Kabul to surrender to the British Envoy Macnaghten. Though the triumphant Suja had no time for the fallen Amir, Macnaghten received him with generous good sense, and sent him off for safe-keeping to Ludhiana in the Punjab.

Three years earlier Shah Suja had been in Ludhiana and Dost Mahomed in Kabul; now their former stations were reversed. It seemed that the East India Company's gamble had paid off : the Army of the Indus had fought its way easily to Kabul; both British and sepoy regiments were pleased with their victories; the Sikhs had put useful pressure on Afghanistan's eastern frontier; finally even Dost Mahomed had placed himself in British hands and had urged his sons to surrender also. Macnaghten and Burnes, as well as Lord Auckland in Calcutta, had every reason for self-congratulation. But their triumph was soon to crumble in their hands.

2

The Occupation

As the Army of the Indus settled into its occupation of Kabul, the problems that confronted both the political officers and the military commanders were a mixture of the trivial and the imponderable. Macnaghten and Burnes had the unenviable task of keeping relations sweet between Shah Suja and his British protectors, as well as trying to ensure that the restored ruler was acceptable to the Afghans. In the interests of Suja's prestige, Macnaghten had stopped the army from repairing and occupying the mighty citadel of Balla Hissar, which dominated Kabul. Suja had complained that if a foreign garrison settled into Balla Hissar this would irreparably damage his standing with his subjects. So the work on the fortress was abandoned, and the British, and ironically Shah Suja, were denied access to an impregnable retreat in the heart of Kabul.

Instead the British troops set to work constructing cantonments on the plain outside Kabul. The site chosen was appalling: it was dominated on all sides by forts and hills, none of which were occupied by the British; between the cantonment and Kabul lay orchards, streams and gardens, all excellent obstacles to the efficient movement of cavalry and field pieces. As if this was not enough, the cantonment, when it was at last constructed, was virtually indefensible; its perimeter was almost two miles long, and there were not enough troops available to defend it properly; to the north was the large Mission Compound, where Envoy Macnaghten and his staff were situated, but which was hardly an extension of the defences; most ludicrous of all was the decision to place the commissariat stores a quarter of a mile outside the cantonment, thus facing the garrison with the possibility of early starvation if a successful uprising was to occur.

These and other examples of military ineptitude were roundly criticized by several British officers, but the commanders, especially the somewhat obtuse Willoughby Cotton, took no heed. One trenchant critic was Brigadier Abraham Roberts, father of a son, Frederick, who would one day become the illustrious Lord Roberts of Kandahar. Abraham Roberts, who had the unenviable task of commanding Shah Suja's shaky levies, pointed out that the lines of communication from Kabul, eastwards to friendly Kandahar and southwards to Ghuznee, were utterly dependent on the goodwill of the local Afghan tribesmen. For the moment the Ghilzyes who dominated these vital routes were co-operating because the East India Company was paying them handsomely to do so, but this was hardly the foundation upon which to build hopes of an orderly and untroubled retreat if that should become necessary.

The criticisms of Roberts and others, including General Sale's son-in-law, fell on unsympathetic ears. Roberts, indeed, was sacked by Macnaghten as a 'croaker' with too much influence in Calcutta. On the surface, to be sure, there was little cause for alarm. The British officers in Kabul remarked on the homosexual proclivities of many Afghan males, and proceeded to seduce their wives and daughters. The British practised an equally vigorous social life beyond the boudoir; they organized horse racing, cock-fighting, wrestling and cricket. The Afghans were, on the whole, pleased to participate in these entertainments – though they drew the line at cricket. British purses were also able to purchase an agreeable range of luxuries, though one effect of this spending spree was to send prices soaring to the detriment of the local Afghans.

Still, the situation seemed so stable by the end of 1839, despite the death of Ranjit Singh and the subsequent lapsing of the Sikh alliance, that Macnaghten, Sale and a host of British officers and men sent for their wives and children. The sepoys of the Company's regiments also sent for their families, and soon it seemed to the wary Afghans that the British forces were preparing for a lengthy occupation. Shah Suja, who had meanwhile surrounded himself with Afghan advisers of extraordinary incompetence and questionable loyalty, also summoned his harem and packed them into the Balla Hissar.

As the year of 1840 drew to its close the British hold on Afghanistan looked, at first sight, firmer than ever. Dost Mahomed had surrendered, and the potentially troublesome region of Khelat (which contained the Bolan Pass) had been annexed by Shah Suja. In January 1841 the blunt and forthright General Nott had routed the Douranee tribes to the north-west of Kandahar. These punitive measures were viewed with equanimity by Envoy Macnaghten, who wrote 'These people are perfect children, and should be treated as such. If we put one naughty boy in the corner, the rest will be terrified.'

Unfortunately the brusque methods of the early-Victorian classroom did not cow the Afghans. Dost Mahomed's deposition was resented enough, Shah Suja's rule unpopular enough, and the British military presence hated enough to keep the cauldron of rebellion bubbling. Major Rawlinson, the Political officer at Kandahar, saw the position clearly when he wrote, 'the state of the country causes me many an anxious thought – we may thrash the Douranees over and over again, but this rather aggravates than obviates the difficulty of overcoming the national feeling against us.'

It had long been obvious to some high-ranking officers that

Shah Suja's authority would collapse the moment the British troops withdrew. But more disturbing still was the conviction that the army of occupation desperately needed reinforcements if it was to maintain its position. General Nott, a Company man, who hated Queen's officers (those seconded from the British regular army for service with the Company's forces) and the Political officers with equal venom, put an outspoken but not unreasonable point of view when he wrote:

> The authorities are never right even by chance, and although most of them are stupid in the extreme, they fancy themselves great men, and even possessed of abilities and talents. They drink their claret, draw large salaries, go about with a numerous rabble at their heels – all well paid by John Bull – or rather by the oppressed cultivators of the land in Hindostan [India]. . . . We are become hated by the people, and the English name and character which two years ago [in 1839] stood so high and fair, has become a byeword. Thus it is to employ men selected by intrigue and patronage! The conduct of the *one thousand and one* politicals has ruined our cause, and bared the throat of every European in this country to the sword and knife of the revengeful Afghan and the bloody Belooch [Baluchi], and unless several regiments be quickly sent, not a man will be left to note the fall of his comrades.

This was strong stuff, and an accurate reflection of Nott's prejudices as well as of his insights. But to be fair, the army was also helping to dig its own grave, even though the first spadefuls had been turned by the diplomats of the Company's political branch. In the spring of 1841 Willoughby Cotton, who had succeeded Sir John Keane in October 1839, retired as commander of the British forces in Afghanistan. The general officer selected to replace Cotton was Major-General William Elphinstone.

Seldom, if ever, can so disastrous a choice have been made in the long history of British arms. Elphinstone (or 'Elphy Bey' as he was nicknamed) was an aristocrat of gentlemanly disposition who, it was reckoned, would get on well with the forceful and opinionated Macnaghten. There the catalogue of his virtues ended for, though renowned for his mild good temper, Elphinstone's military experience was slight and decidedly rusty (he had last seen action upon the field of Waterloo). He found resolute measures well nigh impossible, and preferred to bypass them. He was, moreover, in poor health and limping with gout. As if this was not enough, he was destined to disagree persistently and dangerously with his second-in-command in Afghanistan, the cantankerous, couragous and one-armed Colonel of the 44th Regiment, John Shelton, soon to be promoted Brigadier.

Elphinstone arrived in Kabul in April 1841. Both the political and military chiefs who received him exuded confidence. The outgoing Cotton assured 'Elphy Bey' that 'you will have *nothing to do here, all is peace*'; Macnaghten would not acknowledge the ominous portents that surrounded him. To his credit, one of Elphinstone's first reactions to the army's position in Kabul was to point out the indefensibility of the cantonments and propose a remedy for the deficiency. But the cost of building even a small separate fort was estimated at £2,400 and the Company's rulers in Calcutta would not sanction the expense.

In fact the East India Company had become acutely concerned over the mounting cost of the Afghan enterprise. The Board of Control in Calcutta was appalled at the prospect of spending over a million pounds annually to keep Shah Suja on his throne. Some Company officials were even calling for a complete withdrawal and a drastic cutting of losses. In response to these pressures, Macnaghten took the fateful step of cutting the annual subsidy paid to the Eastern Ghilzyes chieftains to keep the passes to Jalalabad open. As long as they received their £8,000 each year the Ghilzyes had ensured that communications between Kabul and British India were maintained. When Macnaghten announced that the subsidy would be reduced by fifty per cent he unwittingly set terrible events in train. For a saving of a mere £4,000 the Honourable East India Company would have to pay the price of military catastrophe and withdrawal from Afghanistan. William Macnaghten and Alexander Burnes were to pay with their lives.

The Ghilzyes' reaction was prompt. They clamped down on the passes to the east, and plundered the first caravan to come before them. By the start of October 1841, therefore, Kabul was effectively cut off from Jalalabad. Macnaghten, to whom the still grateful Company had just offered the luscious prize of the Governorship of Bombay, was anxious to make light of the difficulties. To demonstrate the settled state of affairs in Afghanistan he now proposed that Robert Sale should march the 1st Brigade back to British India via the Khyber Pass and scatter the insolent Ghilzyes en route. 'Fighting Bob' did indeed force his brigade past the Ghilzyes of the eastern passes and entered Jalalabad on 13 November. But between his departure from Kabul and his arrival at Jalalabad there was a general and ferocious Afghan uprising.

3
The Retreat

Even as 'Fighting Bob' Sale and his brigade were clashing head-
on with the Ghilzyes of the eastern passes, the situation in Kabul
deteriorated. The armed followers of the great men of the city
were giving more or less open aid to the Ghilzyes in their struggle.
British troops were frequently reviled and insulted, and every so
often one would be discovered with his throat cut. Clearly the
Afghans now believed that the British lease was about to expire,
and that the earlier need to cooperate with the 'Feringhees' had
vanished.

By the middle of October 1841 the chiefs in Kabul were preparing to strike a heavy blow at the British. Led by the murderous
Abdullah Khan and the treacherous Amenulah Khan (who was
mistakenly believed to be one of Suja's principal supporters) they
planned to assassinate the British Resident in Kabul, Alexander
Burnes. Burnes had been far unhappier with the British position
than his superior Macnaghten, and had even argued that 'we
shall never settle Afghanistan at the point of a bayonet'. He

hoped, nonetheless, to succeed to Macnaghten's post when the Envoy eventually left to take up the Governorship of Bombay. Burnes never lived to bask in this promotion. On 2 November an angry mob surrounded the Residency, howling for the blood of 'Sekundur' Burnes. The Residency was two miles from the cantonment and though Burnes sent an appeal for help he could hardly have expected any to arrive for several hours. Coolly he harangued the mob in Pushtu, but to no avail. Forced to allow the Residency guard to open fire, Burnes was then persuaded, by a Kashmiri who had wormed his way into the house, to stop the shooting and try to escape in disguise with his younger brother, Lieutenant Charles Burnes. No sooner had the two Britons stepped into the Residency garden than the Kashmiri betrayed them and the mob hacked the two brothers to pieces.

The exhilarated Afghans then sacked the Residency and the house next door belonging to the army Paymaster Captain Johnson. They seized £17,000 of government money and a good deal of loot. They also slaughtered every soldier, servant, woman and child they could find in the two houses. The mob then went off to plunder shops and residences in Kabul. The success of the attack on Burnes brought thousands flocking to join the rioters.

At this point resolute action by the British forces might have contained the situation. Brigadier Shelton was burning to smash the mob, but General Elphinstone vacillated. Half-expecting that the dawn of a new day would bring restored peace, 'Elphy Bey' was equally unable to decide on the best course of action. While Elphinstone dithered, and canvassed opinion, the Afghans captured the hoplessly positioned Commissariat fort, *outside* the cantonment, and laid siege to a second food depot on the outskirts of Kabul and commanded by the fearless Colin Mackenzie. After resisting for two days with his sepoys and Afghan recruits, Mackenzie cut his way out and brought the whole garrison, including women and children, safely to the cantonment.

Mackenzie's heroic action provided an embarrassing counterpoint to Elphinstone's inaction. The Commander of the army of the Indus was prey to devastating physical disabilities as well as mental inertia; he could not walk without great pain, and could hardly ride, so crippled was he with gout. Worse still, he was at the mercy of anybody who offered him advice, from Macnaghten to the humblest junior officer, for he was fatally inclined to think most highly of the opinion last offered him. Thus the Afghans were able to plunder the army's food supplies and still escape retribution, and this in turn encouraged more tribesmen to join the uprising.

Rather than move against the insurgents, Elphinstone was soon urging Macnaghten to consider the benefits of negotiating with them. He held frequent Councils of War at which all could give their views, although the second-in-command, Brigadier Shelton, to show his contempt for 'Elphy Bey', brought his blankets to these conferences and proceeded to fall asleep on the floor !

On 13 November, however, Shelton was given a chance to demonstrate his fighting skills when, on Macnaghten's insistence, he set out to dislodge the Afghans from the Beymaroo hills a few hundred yards north-west of the British cantonments outside Kabul. But Shelton botched the attack, and next day the British infantry was drawn up in two squares on a hill top, with their cavalry behind them, while Afghan warriors, reinforced by artisans from Kabul, picked them off with their jezails. The Afghan jezail, a long-barrelled rifled musket, outranged the smoothbore flintlock muskets of the British. Some jezails were so heavy that they had to be fired from rests, and could hit targets half a mile away. The Afghans also made excellent use of natural cover, and rarely fired unless their jezails were resting properly on some firm support. By contrast Shelton's infantry stood bravely in squares, as if to repulse cavalry, and blazed off indiscriminately at the enemy who were intelligently hidden among the rocky defiles. Soon the Afghans were laughing in derision at the futility of the British stand, and some of them ventured so near the first red-coated square that the officers were forced to pelt them with stones ! At last the troops decided to cut and run, and the fact that so many straggled back to the cantonments was chiefly due to the restraint imposed by the leader of the Afghan cavalry, Osman Khan.

Shelton's humiliating defeat upon the Beymaroo hills, and the news that the tribes to the north of Kabul were also up in arms, had the effect of concentrating Macnaghten's mind wonderfully – though unfortunately the same thing cannot be said for the inert Elphinstone. The Envoy knew that there were several options open to the British in Kabul : they could fight it out, and almost certainly perish; they could capitulate, but this was in principle unthinkable and would, in all probability, have abandoned Shah Suja and the entire British community to torture and barbarous death; finally a withdrawal from Kabul could be negotiated, but with whom, and on what terms? Supported at last by Elphinstone, Macnaghten decided to negotiate.

The first round of negotiations were fruitless; the Afghans arrogantly demanded a complete surrender, the handing over of all arms and ammunition, and the abandonment of Suja who would not, they promised, be killed but merely blinded (though to the Afghans a blind King was as good as dead). Macnaghten, who throughout showed more resolution than many a high-ranking officer, rejected these terms outright. Then at the end of November 1841, Akbar Khan entered Kabul. Akbar was the favourite son of the exiled Dost Mahomed; he was a man of charm, great strength of character and impulsiveness. At first, however, he declined to negotiate, preferring to let hunger and despair further demoralize the British.

Although the commissariat had desperately rounded up a few more days' supplies for the army in Kabul, there was a clear limit to the troops' endurance. Both sepoys and British soldiers were on short rations, the dejected camp followers were stripping the carcases of dead camels, and the horses were being fed on their own dung – having previously stripped the trees of their bark. Moreover, each day brought fresh snow falls, and the sepoys in particular suffered dreadfully from the biting cold.

At last on 11 December, with four days' rations left, Macnaghten met Akbar Khan and a dozen Afghan chieftains and hammered out an agreement. The British garrison at Kabul was to return to India by way of Jalalabad and Peshawur. The garrisons at Ghuznee, Kandahar and Jalalabad itself were to follow them. Dost Mahomed was then to return to Afghanistan, and Shah Suja could leave with the British or stay in peace in Kabul (an unlikely event). The new friendship between Britain and Afghanistan was to be demonstrated by the honour, assistance and, more important, the supplies that were to be vouchsafed for the retreating forces.

But what was the value of such an agreement? The Afghan chiefs were often at each others' throats; Ghazis and Ghilzyes and Barukzyes entertained no permanent mutual affection. Knowing this, Macnaghten still tried to play one group off against the other, until Akbar Khan was convinced of the Envoy's duplicity. Then Akbar lured Macnaghten to a meeting place where, failing to take him as a hostage, he cut him down, and the ferocious Ghazis dismembered the infidel's body. Soon Sir William Macnaghten's hand, stuck upon a pole, was being displayed by the triumphant Ghazis, while his bloody trunk dangled from a meat hook in the bazaar.

The Afghan chieftains now dictated even more humiliating terms to the wretched 'Elphy Bey', including the supply of hostages against Dost Mahomed's safe return, a huge payment of cash, and the abandonment of all but six of the retreating force's horse-drawn guns. Then, in theory, the Kabul garrison would be able to slink like a whipped jackal back to Jalalabad. Given the past manifestations of Afghan treachery, the safe return of these forces was unlikely in the extreme. Lady Sale, the formidable wife of 'Fighting Bob', was quite convinced that 'the chiefs do not mean to keep faith; and it is their intention to get all our women into their possession; and to kill every man except one, who is to have his hands and legs cut off and is to be placed with a letter *in terrorem* at the entrance of the Khyber passes, to deter all Feringhees from entering the country again.'

Nonetheless on 6 January the retreat from Kabul began. It could not have got off to a worse start. Despite the heavy snows, the commanders would not allow their men to swathe their legs and feet in cloth strips (as the Afghans did) and soon after their departure many soldiers were suffering the torture of frost bite. Nor were the troops' bellies packed with food to help keep the cold at bay; for days past the meagre rations had been dispensed, consisting chiefly of small quantities of flour mixed with ghee or dhal. Worse was to follow for, in the confusion of the departure from Kabul, many camp followers threw down their supplies the better to escape from looting Afghans.

The logistics of the situation were hopelessly tilted against the retreating column, for the 4,500 fighting men and more than 12,000 terrified camp followers were expected to march 90 miles through treacherous, snow-filled passes, without fuel or shelter and with very little food. It would have been a daunting prospect in fine weather with benign Afghan tribes to assist the British on their way; as it was there were heavy snows and biting cold, and local tribesmen bent on murder and plunder. Moreover 'Elphy Bey' continued to the last to be wracked with indecision and, when half his force had marched out of the cantonments, he tried to call them back, but was overruled by the courageous Colin Mackenzie and by the contemptuous Shelton.

Of the four and a half thousand soldiers that set out from Kabul, some seven hundred were Europeans (consisting of the Queen's 44th Regiment and a troop of horse artillery). There were nearly a thousand Indian cavalry, three sepoy battalions of the East India Company, several hundred infantrymen from Shah Suja's levies, some sappers and miners, and a few Afghan jezailchis (all expert marksmen, and commanded by Mackenzie).

For seven days the retreating forces straggled through the grim passes of Khoord-Kabul, Tunghee Tareekee and Jugdulluk. Their passage was marked by bloodstained snow and mutilated corpses, for Afghan women and children came to cut up the corpses and dispatch the wounded. The confusion, the deprivation, the despair, were indescribable. Distraught Indian mothers threw their infants from them; sepoys who could not hold their muskets in their frost-bitten hands cast them down and fell prey to the bullets or long knives of the Afghans. At night only a handful of British women and children had any cover, the remainder lay down in the freezing snow and slept as best they could.

Akbar Khan supervised the massacre with a panache flavoured with expressions of regret. He offered Elphinstone's forces supplies, but these never came, though a vital day was spent in waiting. He made a show of offering the Ghilzyes bribes to let the British through. He also scooped up a number of valuable British prisoners and hostages, including Lady Sale, Mackenzie and even Elphinstone, and treated them with forbearance. Fundamentally, however, Akbar wanted the British and their sepoy mercenaries dead.

By 13 January he had almost achieved his ends when a little over fifty men of the 44th struggled through the pass of Jugdulluk and stood at bay at Gandamak. Here the Afghans closed in for the kill, and shot down the exhausted remnants of Elphinstone's force, though six men managed to escape the slaughter. Of this gallant half-dozen only one, surgeon Brydon, evaded his foes, leaving the mutilated remains of his comrades behind him on the road to Jalalabad.

The Afghan campaign had reached its grisly climax; military incompetence and indecisiveness had been unhappily coupled with the inflated optimism of Macnaghten and Burnes, and set against an intractable people inhabiting a bitterly inhospitable terrain. Yet compared with the military resources of the East India Company, the opposition offered by the Afghan tribesmen was trifling. By April 1842, Akbar's forces had been hurled from the gates of Jalalabad, and by 15 September a British Army of Retribution under General Pollock had routed their enemies in pitched battles at Jugdulluk and Tezeen and recaptured Kabul.

The victorious expeditionary force had, however, failed to save Shah Suja from a violent death in March 1842. Elphinstone, too, had died in captivity, worn out with dysentery and haunted by remorse. Other British prisoners were more fortunate, and lived to be reunited with their families and comrades. The exertions of Pollock's men did something to rescue British prestige, but all in all Lord Auckland's 'forward' policy had suffered a crushing defeat and all British forces were withdrawn from Afghanistan. Dost Mahomed was restored to his throne, whence he consistently proved himself an ally of the East India Company, even refusing to support the rebels during the Indian Mutiny of 1857! The ill-fated campaign of 1839–42 was not the last British assault on Afghanistan. In 1878 British forces were once more engaged, and in 1879 General Roberts occupied, and then successfully withdrew from, Kabul. In 1905 the Viceroy of India, Lord Curzon, was unsuccessful in persuading the British government to bring the Afghan Amir to heel with an exacting treaty, and as late as 1919 British and Afghan forces were involved in heavy fighting. In all except the last event, the justification for British involvement lay in the fear of Russian influence over Afghanistan. Yet this 'Russian scare' was for all practical purposes a delusion. The Russian, indeed, could point to much more convincing evidence of British influence in the three invasions of Queen Victoria's reign. The men of the 44th who perished at Gandamak, the sepoys frozen in the snows of Khoord-Kabul, the mutilated Macnaghten and Burnes, were all sacrificed to the phantom of a Russianized Afghanistan, though this does not render their destruction any the less poignant.

Part II
The Crimean War 1854–6

C'est magnifique, mais ce n'est pas la guerre.
General Bosquet on witnessing the charge of the
Light Brigade at Balaclava.

Peace be with him and his hecatomb of twenty thousand
men.
Florence Nightingale when told of Lord Raglan's
death.

4
To the Banks of the Alma

The Crimean War of 1854–6 has become a byword for disaster, gross mismanagement and incompetent leadership. A murky pall of recrimination hangs over it, and even the campaign photographs of Roger Fenton consistently seem to reflect gloom and dirt, and to portray soldiers as creased and grubby pawns depressed by the misfortunes of an ill-fought campaign.

But in fact the British government, through the heroic exertions of the British army and navy and their assorted allies, succeeded at the Peace of Paris of 1856 in its main aim – that of checking Russian expansionist tendencies in the Black Sea, the Balkans and the eastern Mediterranean. Also (for what it was worth) the ailing Turkish empire was maintained as a shaky bulwark against Russian aggression. Nor were the benefits that accrued to Britain merely diplomatic and strategic in character, for out of the scandals of supply and tactics was born a new determination to promote military reform. In the long run, therefore, the common soldier, ill-paid, brutally disciplined and often regarded as a red-coated savage by his superiors, actually benefited from the humiliations and rigours of the campaign.

Given the disgraceful neglect of the British army since the ending of the Napoleonic wars, probably only divine intervention could have averted the exhibition of chaos and indecisiveness in the Crimea. Not that the years between 1815 and 1854 had been barren of British triumphs, as a variety of campaigns in India, southern Africa and New Zealand showed. But these victories had been achieved against non-European forces. Moreover in India the troops raised by the East India Company (both British and sepoy) had borne the brunt of the fighting. In 1854 the British faced neither Kaffirs nor Baluchis, but Russian forces that had recently worsted the Turks in Moldavia and Wallachia, had destroyed the Turkish fleet at Sinope in November 1853, and whose immediate forbears had ripped the heart out of Napoleon's armies in 1812–13. Furthermore the Russian rank and file, though they suffered worse conditions of service than their British counterparts, were fighting for the motherland *in* the motherland and could be counted on to resist ferociously.

The British army that was dispatched to the Crimea in April 1854 was composed of five infantry divisions and one cavalry division. The common foot soldier was poorly paid, fed on monotonous rations consisting mostly of beef broth and potatoes, and packed into a fancy uniform that was well suited to the parade ground but was expected to equally serviceable in tundra, veld and equatorial rain forest. The British infantry were mostly equipped with the effective muzzle-loading Minié rifle, which was replacing the famous 'Brown Bess' muzzle-loader. The Minié rifle was not exclusive to the British; their French allies had it, and so did some of their Russian opponents. In any case, the chief tactic employed on the battlefield was to manoeuvre to within range of the enemy, unleash a volley (or two, with luck) and then close in for hand-to-hand fighting. In these circumstances, the quality of firearm employed was of marginal importance, and the use of cover generally scorned.

In a stand-up fight the quality of tactical military leadership was as important as the endurance and obedience of the rank and file. There were enough recent examples of the British soldier's courage and doggedness to allay misgivings on the latter score, though there was every reason to suppose that the Russians would prove doughty opponents. The quality of the British military command, however, was another matter altogether.

The Duke of Wellington had died in 1852, full of honours, the conqueror of Napoleon and the scourge of chartists and radicals. He was succeeded as Commander-in-Chief by Lord Raglan, whose chief merit lay in his long professional liaison with the Iron Duke. Raglan had served on the Duke's staff, and had subsequently filled the important administrative offices of Secretary-at-War and Master General of the Ordnance. He was sixty-six years of age when Britain entered the Crimean War, and had seen no active service since the Napoleonic Wars. On the field of Waterloo his right elbow had been shattered by a musket-ball, and he had let the surgeon amputate his damaged arm between the shoulder and the elbow without a murmur. As the surgeon tossed the arm away, Raglan called out 'Hey, bring my arm back. There's a ring my wife gave me on the finger.'

So Raglan had an amazingly cool head, proven administrative ability, as well as the best possible social and military connections. Yet for all this, and despite his evident care for the men under his command, Lord Raglan must bear responsibility for the varied disasters of the Crimean campaign. Perhaps, rather like 'Elphy Bey' in Kabul a decade earlier, his tact and even temper were less effective instruments of command than outbreaks of fury or cold sarcasm. Raglan's defects would have mattered less if the commanders of the infantry and cavalry divisions had exhibited first-rate abilities.

Unfortunately, they did not. Only two of the five infantry divisional commanders had led anything larger than a battalion into action against properly trained opponents. Of these five officers, only one was under sixty years of age, and he had never seen action before; this was the Duke of Cambridge, Queen Victoria's cousin, the industrious and affable, though inexperi-

enced commander of the First Division. Sir George de Lacy
Evans, commander of the Second Division, was intelligent, experienced, brusque and fairly radical – probably the ablest of
them all. The Third Division was commanded by the mediocre
Sir Richard England. The Hon. Sir George Cathcart led the
Fourth Division, and was to prove irritable and obstinate under
stress. The Fifth Division was commanded by Sir George Brown,
as brave as a bull, but a renowned flogger, anti-reformer,
martinet, and (in the words of one of his young officers) an 'old
imbecile bully'.

Of the other commanding officers only Sir James Scarlett who
led the Heavy Cavalry Brigade, and the Chief Engineer, the
seventy-two-year-old Sir John Burgoyne, inspired unqualified confidence. Lord Lucan, the commander of the Cavalry Division,
was an obsessional officer with little military experience, though
with enough cash to have once purchased the 17th Lancers for
£25,000 and transformed them into gaudy dandies. His brother-
in-law, Lord Cardigan, led the ill-fated Light Brigade; he was an
arrogant snob who excited even more hatred than Lucan.

There were other disadvantages for the British expeditionary
force. The Commissariat Department of the army was quite in-
adequately staffed to cope with the demands of 30,000 troops
campaigning at the edge of Asia, a fact with which Lord Raglan
was well acquainted from his days as Master General of the
Ordnance. Both the Ordnance and the Commissariat departments were, in any case, responsible to Whitehall, as was the
Army Medical Board. The Commander-in-Chief of the Army
was thus denied control over these essential supports for the fighting man, and was himself accountable to the Secretary-at-War
who was in turn responsible to an overburdened Cabinet minister
the Secretary of State for War and the Colonies.

Inefficient as these administrative relationships were bound to
be under serious stress, they were at least theoretically justifiable
on the grounds that Parliament and Civil Service must stand
between the nation and military dictatorship. Inexcusable, save
on the grounds of penny-pinching, was the decision taken after

1815 to scrap the Waggon Train and the Staff Corps. The Waggon Train had carried essential supplies to places of need during the Napoleonic Wars, and had also acted as an ambulance unit; the Staff Corps had provided some analysis of pressing military problems. The services of both were to be sorely needed in the Crimea.

All in all there was little justification for *The Times'* proud judgement in 1854 that the embarking forces were 'the finest army that has ever left these shores'. The men themselves were soon able to make disturbing comparisons with their French counterparts as the armies gathered along the Dardanelles, at Constantinople and Scutari, and at Varna on the Black Sea coast. So lavish were the medical supplies and equipment that the French possessed that one British officer remarked that they had apparently come to colonize rather than conquer.

To many French officers the British looked absurdly amateurish, and at least fifty years behind the times. Many officers brought their favourite horses, as if to hunt foxes; they also brought servants and tweed suits. Several brought their wives along too. The personal luggage of the British officers astounded the French, and it was noticed that the Duke of Cambridge's baggage filled seventeen carts. Yet despite these comparisons, the British and French troops were naturally anxious to cooperate and made genuine efforts to get along together.

The French forces were divided into four divisions of about 10,000 men each, with eight and a half batteries of field artillery. From the outset they outnumbered their British allies by nearly two to one, and this ratio actually worsened from the British point of view during the campaign. The French armies were led by Marshal St Arnaud, a determined and ambitious man, though in poor health. The four divisional commanders were General Canrobert (nicknamed by the British 'Bob-can't'); Prince Napoleon (nicknamed 'Plon-Plon'), the somewhat fussy cousin of the Emperor Napoleon III; General Bosquet, and General Forey.

Though relations between Raglan and St Arnaud were cordial enough (chiefly due to Raglan's good temper and tact), St

Arnaud considered himself the senior Allied general and early on make a bid for the supreme command by trying to take over the Turkish forces led by the cooperative Omar Pasha. Raglan politely and persistently resisted this move and then proceeded to get the French to agree to an attack on the Russian-occupied territory of the Dobrudja (most of which is now incorporated into modern Romania). The attack was to be based on the Black Sea port of Varna, which was filthy and cramped and sweltering in temperatures of 90° fahrenheit. Soon cholera struck among the Allied armies adding a fearsome partner to the already prevalent diarrhoea.

Still, the very occupation of Varna served its purpose. On 24 June 1854 the Russians abandoned the siege of Silistria in Bulgaria and withdrew across the Danube. Within a few days Turkish armies caught up with them, and by the end of July the provinces of Moldavia and Wallachia had been reconquered.

This Russian retreat neatly fulfilled the declared object of the Allies in going to war; the Turkish Empire was not apparently to be dismembered by the hungry Russian bear after all. It would have been happier for all concerned if the war had stopped here. But the Allied governments were convinced that Sebastopol, the great Russian naval base on the Crimean peninsular, must be taken, and the Russian fleet destroyed. The war was wildly popular in Britain, and the Chancellor of the Exchequer, William Ewart Gladstone, had already raised the rate of income tax from 7d to 1s 2d in the pound. On 14 September the Allied armies made their landfall at Kalamita Bay, thirty-three miles north of Sebastapol.

Between the landing at Kalamita Bay and the Battle of Inkerman on 5 November the Allies achieved considerable success in their encounters with the Russians. This success was all the more remarkable in view of the disagreements between St Arnaud and Raglan, and because cholera continued to plague the advancing armies. The devastations of the deadly disease were sudden and unpredictable; carried in water, the infection can turn a healthy man into a blackened, distorted corpse ready for burning within three or four hours. The Allied commanders did not know, from day to day, whether any of their detachments would be dislocated by cholera. More important still, they did not know the tactics to be employed by the Russian commander-in-chief Prince Menschikov, although his strategy was in theory obvious enough – to defend Sebastopol to the last man.

Equally Raglan and St Arnaud had to press on to Sebastopol, which they did crudely and without finesse. On 20 September the advancing forces came to the river Alma and found the Russian army drawn up on the opposite southern bank. The battle that was joined the next day resulted in an Allied victory, though the fighting revealed serious deficiencies in the high command.

It had all started out bravely enough, and prompted a lyrical description of the Allied advance from a contemporary observer :

> The September sun shone brightly on a forest of bayonets : and while the eye rested with delight on grand and imposing masses of colour, blended yet contrasted, the ear drank in a volume of sound in which the shrill notes of innumerable bugles, and the roll of countless drums, were now lost, now harmonized, in the multitudinous hum of the armed force on the march.

Once Raglan had persuaded the reluctant St Arnaud to agree to a full frontal assault on the Russian positions, however, this parade ground glitter was soon besmirched with blood and dirt.

Almost as soon as the battle opened with an artillery bombardment at 1.30 pm, the Allies were given an unrepeatable chance to scatter the Russians and drive on to Sebastopol. This occurred when the 13,000 French troops on the right flank of the Allied advance made such dramatic and unimpeded progress that they halted, fearful of losing contact with the British on their left. Menschikov, the Russian Commander-in-Chief, chose not to bring up the reserves necessary to contain the French advance; this in turn avoided committing the French fully to the battle. In this way, Menschikov failed to win the Battle of Alma, but in the long run preserved Sebastopol.

Meanwhile the British, on the left flank and in the centre of the line, had advanced head-on against the Russian defensive positions. This was a potentially disastrous gamble, and only paid off due to the heroic efforts of the Highland Brigade, the Light Division and the First Division, the failure of the Russians to make adequate use of their cavalry, and Lord Raglan's decision to bring up the British guns to an untenanted but commanding position in the centre of the battle near Telegraph Hill, where they helped to turn the Russian flank.

But despite this telling initiative, Lord Raglan's command of the battle was open to criticism. Quite apart from the risky frontal assault, he had failed to keep proper contact with his subordinate officers, and there had been an inexplicable confusion over orders when the Guards and Highland Brigades, advancing to take the defensive barrier of the Great Redoubt, had been told to retreat; most detachments obeyed this order but some, like the 7th Fusiliers, did not. Finally Raglan failed miserably to pursue the defeated Russians and turn their retreat into a rout. Of course there were reasons for this inactivity: the French commanders were resentful at being allotted a secondary role in the battle, and refused to chase the Russians; Raglan had every reason to suppose that the Russians, who had only lost six thousand men, were withdrawing in good order and might indeed be luring the Allies into a trap. At any rate, the chance of ending the whole campaign in a matter of weeks was frittered away on the banks of the Alma; moreover, it was only at Balaclava, a month later, that Lords Lucan and Cardigan, who had chafed at the immobility of the cavalry at Alma, were vouchsafed their moment of death or glory.

5
The Valley of Death

The Allied army, numbering some 60,000 men, now moved south towards the Russian citadel of Sebastapol. The subsequent manoeuvres have been the subject of much historical debate, and were passionately argued over by the officers of both sides at the time. Many Russian observers believed that if the Allies had attacked Sebastopol from the north then the town would have fallen easily. Prince Gortschakoff, who had commanded the right wing of the Russian army at the Battle of Alma, later declared 'There was nothing to stop the Allies marching into the town.'

This is an over-simplified view. Sir John Burgoyne, Raglan's chief engineer, considered that the fortifications confronting any advance from the north, though in a state of indifferent repair, were still sufficient to offer a serious obstacle. The French commander St Arnaud, who was about to be fatally stricken with cholera, also advocated skirting the north side of Sebastopol and attacking the town from the south. The opinions of Burgoyne and St Arnaud prevailed and soon the Allied army, with the

British forces in the vanguard, were marching round Sebastopol to the south. This decision was one of the most crucial of the war, since there is strong evidence that an assault from the north would almost certainly have succeeded. Sebastopol would then have fallen, and months of bloody and wasteful siege warfare would have been averted.

Lord Raglan now marched on Sebastopol from the south, using the port of Balaclava as his base. His approach was as brusque and unsubtle as the earlier advance on the Alma. This was unfortunate, because the Russian defences of Sebastopol were in the process of being reorganized by Lieutenant-Colonel Todleben, a military engineer of something like genius. Tirelessly Todleben sited guns, ordered ramparts to be thrown up, and strengthened existing fortifications. There were six main redoubts on the perimeters of Sebastopol : the Quarantine Bastion (nearest to the sea on the west), the Central Bastion, the Flagstaff Bastion, the Redan, the Malakoff, and the little Redan. The Russians worked desperately at these defences, as well as making quite frequent and successful sallies against the advancing Allies. They were also being steadily reinforced by forces drawn from Odessa and other conveniently situated bases. By 9 October, 28,000 fresh troops had entered Sebastopol.

On 25 October 1854 a Russian army of 25,000 foot, thirty-four squadrons of horse, and seventy-eight guns left Sebastopol and advanced towards Balaclava. The Allied forces were drawn up in the following order : the French (now commanded by General Canrobert) on the left flank, and the British on the right; some Turkish detachments manned the redoubts on the Causeway Heights which protected Balaclava.

The Russians pushed on, and achieved early success in the centre by overrunning the foremost Turkish outposts. But then, in the Fedioukine Valley, they found themselves confronted by the 93rd Highland Regiment and the British Cavalry, led by Lucan. The 93rd, inspired by their commander the doughty Sir Colin Campbell with the words 'Remember there is no retreat. You must die where you stand!', did indeed stand firm and turned aside the Russian cavalry. In so doing they inspired *The Times* correspondent, W.H. Russell, to describe them as a 'thin red streak topped with steel.' Thus originated the much mis-quoted phrase the 'thin red line' : it was a description born out of heroism, but also the result of unpreparedness, since it was standard military practice to arrange infantry about to receive cavalry either in squares or in lines four deep. The speed and success of the Russian advance was, more than anything else, responsible for the 'thin red line' at Balaclava.

The 93rd could not, however, check the Russian assault single-handed. This task fell to Lord Lucan's cavalry. The Heavy Brigade, led by General Sir James Scarlett, and consisting of six squadrons, dressed their lines immaculately despite Lord Lucan's repeated orders to charge. The 3,000 Russian cavalry that were pouring over the Causeway Heights halted at the sight of this parade ground display. It seemed absurd that the gaudily dressed British squadrons, numbering a mere 800 men, could stop the Russians, sombre and businesslike in their yellowish-grey overcoats.

At last when Scarlett was satisfied that his ranks were in proper order, he turned and led the charge at the enemy who stood 'as if fascinated, unable to move'. In a flurry of hooves and flashing sabre blades the Scots Greys, Inniskilling Dragoons and the Dragoon Guards crashed into the Russian centre. Such a mass of men were milling and jostling and cursing at the point of impact that the British cavalrymen, hardly able to use their swords in the text-book fashion, hacked at their opponents as if wielding meat-cleavers. After five minutes of desperate fighting the Russian ranks began to waver; their discomfiture was heightened by some British artillery fire falling upon their rear. After eight minutes the Russians broke and fled over the Causeway Heights.

The Heavy Brigade had won an amazing victory against odds of nearly four to one. The troopers' sword arms were weary from hacking and thrusting. Sir James Scarlett had received five sabre cuts, and his dashing aide-de-camp, Lieutenant Elliott, fourteen ! Lord Raglan, who was observing the battle from higher ground, sent a simple but appropriate message, 'Well done, Scarlett.'

The commander of the Light Brigade, Lord Cardigan, who was also watching the fighting from a mere five hundred yards up the valley, commented with a mixture of envy and petulance 'Damn those Heavies, they have the laugh of us this day.' He need not have feared for within a matter of minutes he was to lead one of the most celebrated cavalry charges in British history.

The charge of the Light Brigade at Balaclava became the best remembered incident of the whole Crimean War, nobly assisted in its rise to general acclaim by Alfred Tennyson's verses and generations of subsequent cramming in Board Schools and Public Schools alike. In military terms, however, the charge was one of the least useful or important assaults of the campaign. Its immediate effects were futile, its long-term advantages dubious.

Still, there it is, exerting, even after the passage of more than a century, a fascination over the imagination and providing the material for endless academic debate. It is the classical example of military confusion and ineptitude, infused at the same time with matchless heroism, dash and determination. Some disentangling of the fateful events which led to the charge of the Light Brigade is necessary.

As Lord Cardigan sat at the head of his 673 men watching the triumph of the Heavy Brigade upon the Causeway Heights, his officers were beside themselves with impatience. When the Russian cavalry broke up in confusion, the junior officer temporarily commanding the 17th Lancers rode up to Cardigan and said:

'My Lord, are you going to charge the flying enemy?'

'No, replied Cardigan, 'we have orders to remain here.'

'But, my Lord, it is our positive duty to follow up this advantage.'

'No,' said Cardigan, 'we must remain here.'

'Do, my Lord,' insisted Captain Morris, 'do allow me to charge them with the 17th. Sir, my Lord, they are in disorder.'

'No, no, sir!' snapped Cardigan.

Cardigan afterwards asserted that Lord Lucan's instructions did not enable him to advance at this point in the battle. Lord Lucan, on the other hand, claimed that he had already empowered Cardigan to take advantage of any reasonable opportunity to attack. At any rate, the Light Brigade made no move. Lord Raglan was by now convinced that Cardigan's fresh squadrons should be sent in to hammer home the victory won by the Heavy Brigade. Unfortunately the infantry support that such an attack theoretically required was not forthcoming, though troops of the First Division were moving slowly towards the valley, and Sir George Cathcart's Fourth Division had actually been ordered to advance and capture the redoubts from which the Russians had so recently been driven.

Raglan therefore decided to use the Light Brigade unsupported by infantry. He had little choice but to do so. Lord Lucan had ignored an order issued nearly an hour earlier stating 'Cavalry to advance and take advantage of any opportunity to recover the Heights. They will be supported by the infantry, which have been ordered to advance on two fronts.' There was still no infantry in evidence, and Lord Lucan thus continued to hold his men in check.

While waiting on events, Raglan's staff suddenly saw that Russian horse artillerymen were trying to tow away the abandoned guns on the Heights. A specific new order was now composed. It read: 'Lord Raglan wishes the cavalry to advance rapidly to the front – follow the enemy and try to prevent the enemy carrying away the guns. Troop Horse Artillery may accompany. French cavalry is on your left. Immediate.'

Captain Lewis Nolan was the staff officer chosen to deliver this fateful message. Nolan was selected probably because he was a superb horseman and could ride rapidly down the steep descent into the valley below. In other respects, however, he was far from being the ideal messenger: he was excitable, conceited and priggish, and he openly despised both Lucan and Cardigan. Nolan handed Lucan the order. The cavalry commander read its contents slowly and with mounting consternation, then announced that such an attack would be 'useless'. The fuming Nolan replied: 'Lord Raglan's orders are that the cavalry should attack immediately.'

'Attack, sir!' countered Lucan, 'Attack what? What guns, sir? Where and what to do?'

Nolan waved his arm in a contemptuous gesture down the valley. 'There, my Lord. There is the enemy! There are your guns!'

Lord Lucan was not short-sighted but, denied Lord Raglan's lofty vantage point, all he could see were attended Russian guns massed at the further end of the valley. He rode over to Cardigan and ordered him to advance. Even Cardigan, moustachios bristling, spoiling for a fight, hesitated.

'Certainly, sir,' he replied, 'but allow me to point out to you that the Russians have a battery in the valley in our front, and batteries of riflemen on each flank.'

'I know it,' said Lucan. 'But Lord Raglan will have it. We have no choice but to obey.'

Cardigan turned towards his men, murmuring 'Well, here goes the last of the Brudenells!' He then gave the order to advance. As the men of the Light Brigade trotted down the valley, Captain Nolan, who had stayed to take part in the charge, suddenly dashed before Cardigan, waving his sword and shrieking at him. Probably he realized that the cavalry were heading towards the manned guns not towards the Causeway Heights and was trying to avert disaster. Whatever his motives they brought him a violent death, for a splinter from an exploding Russian shell tore into his chest and killed him.

From various positions, the Allied troops looked on with horror as the Light Brigade was steadily shot to pieces. A torrent of artillery and musket fire poured into their ranks from three sides of the valley. Cardigan rode at the centre, crying 'Close in! Close in! Do look to your dressing on the left!' On every hand his men toppled about him, bodies mutilated, limbs blown off, their horses disembowelled. Eventually the decimated front rank of the British advance reached the Russians guns, and hacked at any of the enemy still in sight. Then, seeing the Russian cavalry drawn up behind the guns, Cardigan turned and trotted back, furious with Captain Nolan's insolence and determined to lodge a complaint.

But even then it was not over. The remaining lines of the Light Brigade broke through past the guns and, seeing at last that they were hopelessly outnumbered, wheeled round and retreated. Of the 673 men who took part in the charge (or trot), 113 were killed and 134 wounded, nearly 500 horses were destroyed, and the gorgeous uniforms of this elitist brigade were besmirched with grime and soaked in blood.

The charge of the Light Brigade was, of course, a disaster : splendid, heroic, but grotesquely contravening standard military practice. Compared with later losses sustained by British forces, during the Great War, for example, the death of 113 out of 673 does not seem excessive. The fame or notoriety of the assault owes much more to the confusion over the order transmitted from Lord Raglan via Captain Nolan. Lord Raglan can hardly be blamed for this. Nor, in a sense, can Lords Lucan and Cardigan, though both (especially Lucan) could have exercised more discretion – after all, there were several examples of straightforward refusals to obey orders during the campaign. Nolan, unfortunately, could bear no witness.

Raglan was incensed at the catastrophe, but tried to shield Lucan from official criticism. Cardigan was quite unrepentant, and rode from the field of battle to take a bath, consume a bottle of champagne, and go to bed. It was not long before he left the Crimea at his own request. Lucan was simply recalled.

The final tragedy of the wasteful yet heroic charge of the Light Brigade was that it did nothing to win the battle and, arguably, lost it. The Russian advance on Balaclava had been halted. But they still occupied the Causeway Heights, and commanded the vital Woronzoff road, possession of which would have allowed the British to move supplies easily from Balaclava and would have thus averted some of the horrors of the coming winter.

6
Before Sebastopol

Having been worsted at the Battle of Alma, and having gained the upper hand at Balaclava, the Russians now moved against the Allies at Inkerman, aiming to turn their recent advantage into overwhelming success. There was every reason why they could hope to achieve just that; their forces amounted to 55,000 with 220 guns; the Allies, though they numbered 63,000, were unable to concentrate more than 16,000 for the approaching battle.

The Russians attacked in two columns, totalling 35,000 men and supported by over 100 guns, on 5 November 1854. Ironically Lord Raglan had just succeeded in persuading the French to move against Sebastopol on 7 November. Now he was to be the one under attack. At 5 am, shrouded by fog, the Russian guns opened fire and the Russian advanced infantry columns clashed with the men of the British Second Division commanded by General Pennefather. The Second Division straddled, like the other British forces, diagonally across Inkerman Ridge did not withdraw but counter-attacked sharply. Somewhat disconcerted, the Russians, who heavily outnumbered the forces ranged immediately opposite them, withdrew.

The Russian commander Soimonoff then threw 9,000 men at the centre of the British line of defence. They were caught in an uncomfortable flank fire from the 77th Foot, and eventually driven back after ferocious hand-to-hand fighting in which General Soimonoff and several of his staff were killed.

One Russian column had thus been dispersed, but the second, under General Pauloff, was making better headway until faced with an unexpected bayonet charge by a mere two hundred men of 30th Foot. The Russians fell back. Yet another Russian attack was contained by men of the Fourth Division and the Brigade of Guards. More Russian forces, led by General Dannenberg, pounded away at the Allied centre. Though French units were now engaged, the Allies continued to be grossly outnumbered, but their eighteen-pounder guns were able to concentrate their fire on the narrow Russian front, with devastating results.

Eventually after very costly bouts of hand-to-hand fighting which left 'the field of battle ... a terrible sight, near a battery round where there was a great struggle the bodies lie so thickly one can hardly walk', the Russians retreated. The Allies had won the Battle of Inkerman, against the odds, though at the cost of 2,573 killed and wounded. The Russians, on the other hand, had lost nearly 15,000 of whom close on 5,000 were left dead on the battlefield; these were grievous casualties even though the Russians could obviously bring up replacements far more easily than the Allies.

Still, the enemy continued to hold Sebastopol and the grim Russian winter was closing round the Crimea. Neither side looked to be on the point of winning the war. The siege of Sebastopol dragged on through the winter, spring came, and the summer; finally in September 1855, after the French had captured the Malakoff and the British had failed to hold the Redan, the Russians evacuated the city, and peace negotiations began in earnest, resulting in the Treaty of Paris in February 1856. Nearly a year of hard slogging had produced no great Allied victories won by zestful troops in bright-coloured uniforms. Heroic confrontations there had certainly been, but mainly fought according to the conservative conventions of siege warfare, amid the stench of diarrhoea and putrefying corpses, with cholera striking with no regard for rank or station, and with dirt and dishevelment the lot of the common soldier.

The British forces on the Crimea lost 18,058. Of these, only 1,761 died due to enemy action, the rest died of disease. The vast majority of those who died of disease (16,297) were stricken during the first nine months of the war, when the mortality rate among some units reached a staggering sixty per cent. It is small wonder that the deficiencies of supply and medical care raised such a storm of criticism at home, that even the inadequacies of Lord Raglan and his subordinates went unchallenged by comparison.

From the outset of the campaign it was recognized that all ranks faced conditions of rare harshness. W. H. Russell, *The Times* correspondent, wrote:

> The oldest soldiers never witnessed or heard of a campaign in which general officers were obliged to live out in tents on the open field, for the want of a roof to cover them, and generals who passed their youth in the Peninsular War, and who had witnessed a good deal of fighting since that time in various parts of the world, were unanimous in declaring that they never knew or read of a war in which officers were exposed to such hardships. They landed without anything but what they could carry, and they marched beside their men, slept by them, fought by them, and died by them, undistinguished from them in any respect, except by the deadly epaulet and swordbelt, which have cost so many lives to this country. The survivors were often unable to get their things from on board ship. They laid down at night in the clothes which they wore during the day; many delicately nurtured youths never changed shirt and shoes for weeks together, and they were deprived of the use of water for ablution, except to a very limited extent.

There was much worse to come, even for less delicately

nurtured youths, when the battles began and when winter struck. Men took all sorts of rough and ready devices to keep out the cold. Some put:

> long stockings outside their rags or trousers; some had garters made from old knapsacks; others had leggings made from sheepskins, bullocks' hides, horse hides – anything to keep out the extreme cold. . . . Our men's coats were nothing but rags tacked together. As for head dress some had mess tin covers that could be pulled down well over the ears; others had coverings for the head made out of old blankets four or five times doubled. . . . Some of their beards and moustaches were almost two inches long, and sometimes these were so frozen that they could not open their mouths until they could get a fire to thaw them.

But the worst horrors were reserved for the wounded, or those suffering from disease. Quite early in the campaign it was evident that hospital facilities were appallingly inadequate. At the hospital at Balaclava nurse Elizabeth Davis recalled:

> I began to open some of their wounds. The first that I touched was a case of frost bite. The toes of both the man's feet fell off with the bandages.
>
> The hand of another fell off at the wrist. It was a fortnight, or from that to six weeks, since the wounds of many of those men had been looked at and dressed. . . . One soldier had been wounded at Alma. . . . His wound had not been dressed for five weeks, and I took at least a quart of maggots from it. From many of the other patients I removed them in handfuls.

Some of the sick and wounded must be accounted lucky even to have got as far as a filthy verminous and overcrowded hospital. At Balaclava, Mrs Duberly, the wife of an officer of the 8th Hussars, recorded her impressions in her journal:

> I hear the sick are dying at an average of eighty per diem. With some horror (not much) and a great deal of curiosity, I watched from over the taffrail of the Star of

the South the embarkation of some Russian prisoners and English soldiers (all wounded) for Scutari. The dignified indifference of the medical officer, who stood with hands in his pockets, gossiping in the hospital doorway – the rough, indecent way in which the poor howling wretches were hauled along the quay and bundled, some with one, and others with both legs amputated, into the bottom of the boat, without a symptom of a stretcher or bed, was truly an edifying exemplification of the golden rule 'Do to others as you would be done by'.

Soon letters were reaching horrified relatives in Britain, as when Captain Godman of the 5th Dragoon Guards wrote of the shipment of wounded to the hospital at Scutari, opposite Constantinople on the Bosphorous:

I believe you think in England that every preparation has been taken to make the sick and wounded as comfortable as possible. Such is not the case. Indeed anything so disgraceful as the whole department it is impossible to imagine. The other day I was told on good authority that 500 men went to Scutari after Alma, sick and wounded in one ship, and attended by two surgeons and five men, one of whom died on the way, and the poor fellows had no one to assist them or look after them. On their arrival no preparations for their reception had been made. There are 1,200 wounded at Scutari, and 4,000 in hospital altogether there. I heard from one hospital sergeant who went on board one of the ships at Balaclava the other day that the state of things there is just as bad or worse, the ship crowded with men shouting for water, and no one to attend them.

It was at Scutari that Florence Nightingale battled as valiantly as any soldier in the field to improve conditions so vile as to defy description. The men were piled up in corridors, lying on unscrubbed, rotting floors crawling with vermin. In the wards there were at first no screens behind which the doctors could carry out the brisk and grisly business of amputation, which was almost the only kind of surgery performed. In Florence Nightingale's early days in the hospital at Scutari there were more than a thousand patients suffering from acute diarrhoea and only twenty chamber pots to go round! The privies were blocked up and an inch of liquid filth floated over the floor. Furthermore, 'The majority of the cases at the Barrack Hospital were suffering from diarrhoea, they had not slippers and no shoes, and they had to go into this filth so that gradually they did not trouble to go into the lavatory chamber itself.' The men's food often lay in this revolting mess. It was small wonder that Florence Nightingale wrote despairingly, 'We have Erysipelas, fever and gangrene . . . the dysentery cases have died at the rate of one in two . . . the mortality of the operations is frightful. . . . This is only the beginning of things.' The vile stench from the hospital penetrated the walls and could be smelt from some distance away.

The British public were searching furiously for a scapegoat during the winter of 1854–5. Who was to blame? That 'old traitor Aberdeen' (the Prime Minister)? Lord Raglan? His Staff? The Secretary of State for War (the Duke of Newcastle)? Queen Victoria put her own misgivings before Lord Raglan in a reasonable but concerned letter written on 1 January 1855:

> The sad privations of the Army, the bad weather and the constant sickness are causes of the deepest concern and anxiety to the Queen and the Prince. The braver her noble Troops are and the more patiently they bear all their trials and sufferings the more miserable we feel at their long continuance.
>
> The Queen trusts that Lord Raglan will be very strict in seeing that no unnecessary privations are incurred by any negligence of those whose duty it is to watch over their wants. The Queen heard that their coffee was given them green instead of it being roasted and several other things of the kind. It has distressed the Queen as she feels so conscious that they should be made as comfortable as circumstances can admit of. The Queen earnestly trusts that the larger amount of warm clothing has not only reached Balaclava but has been distributed and that Lord Raglan has been successful in procuring the means of

hutting for the men. Lord Raglan cannot think how much we suffer for the Army and how painfully anxious we are to know that their privations are decreasing.

Lord Raglan replied directly telling the Queen that he could

with truth assure your Majesty that his whole time and all his thoughts are occupied in endeavouring to provide for the various wants of your Majesty's troops. It has not been in his power to lighten the burden of their duties. . . . Much having been said, as Lord Raglan has been given to understand, in private letters, of the inefficiency of the staff, he considers it to be due to your Majesty, and a simple act of justice to those individuals, to assure your Majesty that he has every reason to be satisfied with their exertions, their indefatigable zeal, and undeviating close attention to their duties.

On the other hand, Raglan was very much aware of deficiencies in medical care and supply. In December 1854 he issued a General Order that was highly critical of the treatment of the sick and wounded :

The Commander of the Forces is sorry to have to animadvert very strongly upon the conduct of the medical department, in an instance which came under his observation yesterday. The sick went down from the camp to Balaclava under the charge of a medical officer of the division to which they respectively belonged; but on their arrival there it was found that no preparations had been made for their reception. The Commander of the Forces is aware that Deputy Inspector-General of Hospitals Doctor Dumbreck gave the necessary order verbally to the staff medical officer at Balaclava, but that officer neglected to inform his superior and the consequence was that the sick, many of them in a very suffering state, remained in the streets for several hours, exposed to the very inclement weather. The name of the officer who was guilty of this gross neglect is known to the Commander of the Forces. He will not now publish it, but he warns him to be careful in future, and to be cautious how he again exposes himself to censure. Doctor Dumbreck will, in future, give his orders in writing, addressed to the responsible officer. When a convoy of sick is sent from the camp either to the hospitals, or to be placed on board ship, it is henceforth to be accompanied not only by a medical officer, but likewise by the DAQMG of the Division, who will precede it to the place of deposit, and take such steps as may ensure the due reception and care of the men confided to his charge.

But Lord Raglan's censorious interventions could not halt the flood of private and public criticism. Towards the end of December 1854 a *Times* leader thundered:

There are people who think it a less happy consummation of affairs that the Commander-in-Chief and his staff should survive alone on the heights of Sebastopol, decorated, ennobled, duly named in despatch after despatch, and ready to return home to enjoy pensions and honours amid the bones of fifty thousand British soldiers, than that the equanimity of office and the good-humour of society should be disturbed by a single recall or a new appointment over the heads now in command.

Lieutenant-Colonel Anthony Sterling, who served in the Crimea, later published *The Story of the Highland Brigade in the Crimea*, in which he expressed a variety of hard-hitting judgements on the conduct of the war. He attacked the 'gossip' of British journalists in the Crimea and also the rapid promotion vouchsafed to the aristocratic officers of the elitist Guards Regiments. But he also had more general and more telling criticisms:

The mistake that has been made has been a very common one in our country, viz, not keeping up certain military establishments in peace, because people took it into their heads that war would never come. In France there is a permanent waggon-train always organized, a permanent commissariat, and also a permanent ambulance; these three departments hang very much upon one another. The English people having destroyed these above-named departments, which existed during the Spanish War, or which rather were then formed, its Government, on deciding upon war, should have instantly begun to organize them again. This is a matter of time as well as money; there has now been time enough allowed to slip away; but nothing is really organized yet.

And this when our army belongs, not only to the richest country in the world, but to the country richest in horses and ships. Many of the Staff and general officers were appointed from interest. It seemed either that Lord Raglan did not expect war, and so gave places to anyone who had influence, or if he did expect war, he intended to do all the work himself. . . . Escourt was pitch-forked into the important office of adjutant-general, with high pay and powers; but his business is discipline, which he endeavours to combine with amiability; a most charming man in private life, but quite out of place here.

The huge volume of criticism and complaint had its effect. In February 1855 the Aberdeen government fell; the bellicose Lord Palmerston became Prime Minister and Lord Panmure went to the War Office. The new administration were determined to make drastic improvements in the running of the war and to overhaul the management of military affairs as a whole. This resulted in a steady improvement in the organization and administration of the British army, which emerged from the war a substantially modernized force. The French, on the other hand, who had not suffered such acute catastrophies of supply and organization as the British, did not carry out equivalent reforms.

Lord Raglan was not sacked as some had advocated. He remained as Commander-in-Chief until June 1855, when he was stricken with illness, and died, a few days after his much criticized Adjutant-General, J.B. Escourt. It was swiftly rumoured that Raglan, who had remained patient, kindly and considerate to the end, had died of a broken heart. 'It was not *cholera*', wrote Florence Nightingale from Scutari, 'the diarrhoea was slight but he was so *depressed*', and this explanation, though perhaps inadequate in medical terms, is a fitting epitaph.

Part III
The Indian Mutiny 1857–9

We must not forget that in the sky of India, serene as it is, a small cloud may arise, at first no bigger than a man's hand, but which growing larger and larger, may, at last, threaten to burst, and overwhelm us with ruin.

Lord Canning, Governor-General designate speaking in London in 1856.

It is difficult to resist the conclusion that the affair was a muddle, however gloriously conducted, from beginning to end.

Captain Maude, Royal Artillery, after the relief of Lucknow.

7
'The Devil's Wind': the Mutiny Begins

As the British forces struggled in the toils of the Crimea, the Shah of Persia had taken the opportunity once more to lay siege to Herat in western Afghanistan. The British East India Company, still acutely sensitive to Persian, and hence possibly Russian, influence in Afghanistan decided, with the backing of the British government, to invade Persia early in 1857. A brief campaign ended with a conclusive victory for the Company's forces. On 29 May Brigadier-General Henry Havelock, one of the victorious divisional commanders, sailed into Bombay harbour in the steamship *Berenice* 'in time to receive the astounding intelligence that the Native regiments have mutinied at Meerut, and that the fortress of Delhi was in the hands of the mutineers, whilst disaffection seemed everywhere spreading in the Upper Provinces'.

It is, of course, impossible to estimate how far the absence of large numbers of troops in Persia, or British difficulties in the

Crimea, helped to cause the Mutiny of 1857. The sepoys in the Company's regiments would have known of the successive failures to take Sebastopol, but equally they would have received news of the earlier victories of Alma and Inkerman. Moreover, although the campaign in Persia had removed substantial numbers of European troops from India, the triumphant outcome of the invasion meant that these forces could be hustled back to deal with the Mutiny.

In fact, the roots of the uprising went far deeper. The territorial annexations and reforming tendencies of the East India Company had affronted many sections of Indian society in the half century since the victorious conclusion of the Maratha Wars in 1818 had unquestionably established the British as the paramount power in the sub-continent. For the vast majority of the Indian people it was probably irrelevant whether the Mogul Emperor, the Maratha Confederacy or the Honourable East India Company ruled them; the timeless struggle for subsistence was their overwhelming preoccupation. Peasant India, fatalistic and passive, was an unlikely recruiting ground for bloodstained revolutionaries.

Princes, landlords, religious leaders, and members of the upper reaches of Hindu and Muslim society saw things differently. The East India Company had toppled Indian rulers, dispossessed landlords, and had seemed to encourage attacks on the indigenous religious and cultural order. The proselytizing of evangelical Christian missionaries, the abolition of *suttee* (the burning of Hindu widows) and the passing of laws permitting the remarriage of such widows, the attempt to stamp out the thugs, who robbed and strangled travellers as sacrifices to the goddess Kali, all seemed to be part of the Company's programme to subvert the Indian tradition.

The governor-generalship of Lord Dalhousie (1848–56) intensified resentments that had been building up for many years. Dalhousie confidently asserted the paramountcy of the Company, thus also implying the superiority of British ways over Indian. His plans to improve road and rail communications were justified in terms of military security but seemed further, perturbing, examples of change to Indian traditionalists. Above all, Dalhousie's unashamed policy of territorial annexation was bound to alienate fallen rulers and their followers. As the climax to his series of annexations, Dalhousie brought the ancient province of Oudh under the Company's rule in 1856. Oudh, rich, fertile and densely populated was the last great independent province in northern India. It lay between Bengal and the Punjab, straddling the grand trunk road from Calcutta to Delhi, the Ganges and the Jumna rivers, and the newly completed railway link between Allahabad and Cawnpore. In 1837 the Company had guaranteed the province's independence, but Dalhousie's annexation in 1856 was justified on the not unreasonable grounds of endemic civil disorder. A more compelling justification was that Oudh had become an anachronistic obstacle to the Company's plans for territorial and military aggrandizement throughout the whole of the Ganges valley.

The significance of the annexation of Oudh lay not only in its strategic importance, but also in the fact that 40,000 sepoys (nearly a third) in the Army of Bengal had been recruited from the province. The East India Company maintained three armies, those of Bengal, Madras and Bombay. At the beginning of 1857 there were 45,522 European troops in India, consisting of 4 regiments of cavalry, 31 regiments of infantry and 64 batteries of artillery – some of which had Indian personnel. There were 232,224 sepoys serving in the three armies, of which 151,000 composed the Army of Bengal.

In general, the sepoys of the Bengal Army were drawn from the more exalted sections of Indian society: Brahmins and Rajputs if they were Hindus, or good class Muslim families if followers of Islam. On donning their uniforms they did not become mere tools of Company policy; they maintained their religion, their caste, and the family connections. Their unbroken links with their families had a twofold significance: one was that they were particularly sensitive to any fears or resentments that affected their families; the other was that they had an important status to maintain in the eyes of their relatives. Any slight to their religion, any threat to their caste or standing, would have resulted in rejection by family and friends.

The fifty years before the Mutiny had seen other military insurrections. In 1806 and 1824 sepoys had feared that the Company was undermining their religions; both mutinies had been ferociously suppressed. As late as 1852, a regiment had refused service in Burma, since crossing the sea would have involved its Hindu troops in a loss of caste; this regiment had been simply diverted to other duties. But early in 1857 dark rumours began to circulate concerning the issue of a new cartridge.

The Company had decided to equip its sepoy regiments with the Enfield rifle in place of the smooth-bored 'Brown Bess' musket. The rifled barrel of the new weapon necessitated a greasing of the cartridges in order to ram home easily the rifle bullet that was placed in the base of each cartridge. The loading procedure for these new 'balled' cartridges was as follows: first tear off the top of the cartridge; then pour the gunpowder down the rifle barrel; finally ram the empty container with its bullet down the rifle. It seems clear that between 1847 and 1857 there had been a wholesale changeover to 'balled' cartridges. Hitherto the 'unballed' cartridges had simply been thrown away, and the bullet taken from a separate pouch.

The fateful implication of this military change was that the sepoys came to believe that the grease on the cartridges was made from animal fat. To the Hindu the cow was a sacred animal, the Muslim believed that contact with the unclean pig would defile him. In January 1857 sepoys near the great Dum-Dum arsenal close to Calcutta became convinced that the new-issue cartridges were coated with cow and pig fat. Their suspicions seem to have been well-founded. That such a thing could happen indicates either blind stupidity on the part of the military authorities or gross negligence. Frederick Roberts, who fought against the Mutiny and won the Victoria Cross, and was later to become Field-Marshal Lord Roberts of Kandahar, subsequently wrote:

'The cartridge was actually composed of the objectionable in-gredient's cow's fat and pig's lard; and incredible disregard of the sepoy's religious prejudices was displayed in the manufacture of these cartridges.'

In general there were genuine causes for discontent among the Company's Indian troops, whether sepoys (foot soldiers) or sowars (cavalrymen). The strains of barrack life and the demands of military routine and discipline could in themselves foment a spirit of sullen resentment, especially if British officers were unable to maintain close and cordial relationships with their men. There is a good deal of evidence to show that a wide gulf between officers and sepoys had in fact opened up prior to the Mutiny. An Indian officer in the Company's service, Subedar Sita Ram, who later published a book entitled *From Sepoy to Subedar*, recalled of the immediate pre-Mutiny period: 'I always was good friends with the English soldiery, and they formerly used to treat the sepoys with great kindness ... these soldiers are of a different caste now – neither so fine nor so tall as they were; they seldom can speak one word of our language, except abuse.' A British observer, writing in 1857 from his experience in the mutiny-torn North West Provinces, said of the British treatment of the sepoy: 'He is sworn at. He is treated roughly. He is spoken of as a "nigger". .... The younger men seem to regard it as an excellent joke, and as evidence of spirit and as a praiseworthy sense of superiority over the sepoy to treat him as an inferior animal.'

Lord Roberts was equally damning when he wrote:

> That long-existing discontent and growing disloyalty in our Native Army might have been discovered sooner and grappled with in a sufficiently prompt manner to put a stop to the mutiny, had the senior regimental and staff officers been younger, more energetic and intelligent, is an opinion to which I have always been strongly inclined. Their excessive age, due to a strict system of promotion by seniority which entailed the employment of Brigadiers at

seventy, Colonels of sixty, and Captains of fifty must have prevented them from performing their duties with energy and activity.

Though it must be made plain that Roberts himself was only twenty-five years of age when the Mutiny broke out and a mere Lieutenant, his strictures had great force in them, and merely confirmed the judgement of the former Governor-General, Lord Bentinck, that the Bengal Army was 'the most expensive and inefficient in the world.'

At any rate, the Army of Bengal was about to be shaken by a series of disturbances beginning in February 1857. First affected was the cantonment at Barrackpore, close to Calcutta, which was the main centre of Company power. Here sepoys of the 2nd Native Infantry objected to the cartridges recently sent from Dum-Dum. The British commanders held a Court of Enquiry and discovered the depth of the genuine revulsion against the greased cartridges. On 9 February, Major-General Hearsey, the Commander of the Presidency Division, paraded the whole brigade at Barrackpore and assured them in Hindustani that there was no European plot to convert them forcibly to Christianity. This sensible exercise in public relations was not, alas, imitated elsewhere.

A few days later trouble broke out at Berhampore, further up the Ganges. Again the new cartridges were the source of sepoy discontent, and brought about a knife-edge confrontation between Lieutenant-Colonel Mitchell and men of the 19th Native Infantry. Mitchell tried to bully his Indian officers and break the will of the sepoys, but it was he who eventually backed down and withdrew the guns and cavalry with which he hoped to overawe his native troops. A Court of Inquiry at Berhampore disclosed that rumours over the cartridges had been circulating for at least two months previously. The Company decided to disband the 19th Native Infantry, and this order was carried out on 31 March at Barrackpore; the disgraced regiment was paraded before the other troops in the station, made to pile up their arms, belts, bayonets and colours, and sent off to Chinsurah. The authorities, however, were still determined to be as moderate as possible. The 19th Native Infantry were paid, transport was provided for them and their families, and after another address from the multi-lingual Hearsey, they marched off, lustily cheering their old commander.

But three days before this episode, a more menacing incident had occurred at Barrackpore. A Brahmin sepoy of the 34th Native Infantry called Mangal Pande, probably intoxicated with hemp and certainly intent on causing a furore, had called on his comrades to come out and help him defend their threatened religion. While resisting arrest, Mangal Pande wounded the regimental Sergeant-Major and the Adjutant before he was briskly and bravely disarmed by Major-General Hearsey himself. Pande was court martialled, and hanged on 21 April, and the 34th partially disbanded on 6 May.

These were not unreasonable punishments in an age when British troops could be given a hundred lashes for fairly trivial offences. After all, Mangal Pande had tried to incite mutiny. But the significance of the train of events lay in the suspicion that Pande had merely spoken unspeakable things on behalf of the vast majority of his comrades who had failed, in the last resort, to back him up. The executed Pande, the disbanded 19th and 34th regiments, became martyrs for the sepoys of the Bengal Army, and the punishments meted out serve to inflame opinion rather than act as a deterrent. Many British officers now faced the terrifying prospect of a mass uprising of thousands of 'pandies' (the anglicized term of abuse for the imitators of Mangal Pande) throughout the length of the Ganges valley, and possibly beyond.

Short of annihilation on the field of battle, a general mutiny is the most disastrous misfortune to befall any army. By the beginning of May 1857 the Army of Bengal teetered on the brink of such a catastrophe, and the causes and implications of the impending disaster were almost uncannily defined in a letter written

F

early in that month by Captain Martineau of the Musketry Depot at Ambala, some 120 miles north of Delhi:

> Feeling . . . is as bad as can be and matters have gone so far that I can hardly devise any suitable remedy. We make a grand mistake in supposing that because we dress, arm and drill Hindustani soldiers as Europeans, they become one bit European in their feelings and ideas. I see them on parade for say two hours daily, but what do I know of them for the other 22?
>
> What do they talk about in their lines, what do they plot? For all I can tell I might as well be in Siberia.
>
> I know that at the present moment an unusual agitation is pervading the ranks of the entire native army, but what it will exactly result in, I am afraid to say. I can detect the near approach of the storm, I can hear the moaning of the hurricane, but I can't say how, when, or where it will break forth.
>
> Why, whence the danger, you say. Everywhere far and near, the army under some maddening impulse, are looking out with strained expectation for something, some unseen invisible agency has caused one common electric thrill to run thro' all.
>
> I don't think they know themselves what they will do, or that they have any plan of action except of resistance to invasion of their religion and their faith.
>
> But, good God! Here are all the elements of combustion at hand, 100,000 men, sullen, distrustful, fierce, with all their deepest and inmost sympathies, as well as worst passions, roused, and we thinking to cajole them into good humour by patting them on the back, saying what a fool you are for making such a fuss about nothing. They no longer believe us, they have passed out of restraint and will be off at a gallop before long.
>
> If a flare-up from any cause takes place at one station, it will spread and become universal.

The flare-up occurred at Meerut on 10 May, and the flames lit on that fateful day were soon threatening to devour the very fabric of the Company's authority from Calcutta to the Punjab. Oddly, Meerut seemed a most unlikely place for an insurrection, since the European and Indian troops in the garrison were of almost equal numbers. Nor was it the only trouble spot in those tense days, for a week before the outbreak at Meerut the 7th Oudh Irregular Native Infantry stationed at Lucknow refused to bite the offensive cartridge and were promptly disbanded by the vigilant Sir Henry Lawrence, Chief Commissioner for Oudh.

Men of the 3rd Native Light Cavalry at Meerut also refused to use the greased cartridges on 23 April. A court martial, composed of Indian officers, sentenced eighty-five of them to ten years of hard labour. Despite rumblings of protest among the sepoys and sowars at Meerut, and the tireless work of barrack-room agitators, the garrison might have avoided bloodshed but for the decision of the divisional commander Major-General ('Bloody Bill') Hewitt to publicly humiliate the convicted men. On 9 May, shackled with leg-irons, the mutineers shuffled before their comrades, appealing to them for help. That night the sepoy regiments rose in rebellion, released the prisoners from jail, burned down bungalows and offices, and killed any Europeans that fell into their hands. Then they set off for Delhi, thirty-six miles away to the south-west.

It was at this point that resolute action by the remaining British officers of the Meerut garrison might well have stemmed the rising tide of mutiny and disaffection. Not all of the sepoys at Meerut had rebelled, and it was likely that if European and loyal Indian troops had pursued the mutineers to Delhi they might have prevented the fall of the city. A young company officer Hugh Gough (later to become General Sir Hugh Gough) was in no doubt as to the failure of British nerve at this crucial point :

> strange to say, not a movement had as yet been made for either succour or vengeance. There appeared to be a general paralysis. General Hewitt was a very old officer, and on this occasion was completely unmanned. He had more or less relegated his authority to Brigadier Archdale

Wilson. . . . Major Rosse of the Carabiniers . . . had earnestly implored the brigadier to allow him to take his squadron and a couple of horse-artillery guns and pursue the mutineers – even to the walls of Delhi. I have always been firmly convinced had it been carried out, Delhi would have been saved.

But Delhi was not saved. There were no European regiments in the city, and the sepoys there were only too ready to welcome the Meerut mutineers with open arms. Lieutenant Edward Vibart was an eyewitness to these events, and wrote :

The orderly havildar of my company came running up to my bungalow to report that the regiment had received orders to march down instantly to the city, as some troopers of the 3rd Light Cavalry had that morning arrived from Meerut and were creating disturbances. Hurrying on my uniform, and ordering my pony to be saddled, I without loss of time galloped down to the parade-ground, and saw the regiment falling in by companies and preparing to start.

But soon the sepoys turned ferociously on their British officers :

Killed were poor Burrowes, Smith, Edwards, and Water-field, all of my own regiment. The fifth was one of the European sergeants attached to the corps; he was the only one alive. A ball had shattered his leg, and he had another frightful wound on his head. Since then I have witnessed many painful sights, but I shall never forget my feelings that day as I saw our poor fellows being brought in, their faces distorted with all the agonies of a violent death, and hacked about in every conceivable way. . . .

Reports now reached us that, besides the 3rd Cavalry troopers, two regiments of native infantry, the 11th and 20th, had also arrived from Meerut, and were on their way to attack us. . . .

In this state of disquieting suspense, the first hour passed by, and we were speculating on the possible fate of the rest of the officers of the 54th, when, to my great joy, Lieutenant Osborn, our Adjutant, and Captain Butler suddenly made their appearance. The latter was besmearched with blood, and was faint from a blow he had received on the head from a large brickbat. We now learnt some particulars of the events of the morning.

It appeared that no sooner had the regiment advanced through the Kashmir Gate into the open space in front of the church, than they were assailed by about twenty troopers dressed in uniform. These men shouted out to the sepoys that they had no intention of hurting them, but had merely come to slaughter the accursed Feringhees (English). Our officers were then sabred and shot down. Vainly they called on their men to fire on the troopers: these miscreants, on the contrary, immediately joined with the insurgents, and some of the cowardly traitors actually bayoneted Colonel Ripley after he was unhorsed and cut down.

By now the chief concern of the British officers in Delhi was to save the magazine and arsenal from falling into rebel hands. A handful of Britons defended the magazine until their last round had been fired. Then in the words of one of them, Lieutenant Forrest:

Lieutenant Willoughby gave the signal for firing the magazine. Conductor Scully, who had from the first evinced his gallantry by volunteering for this dangerous duty, now coolly and calmly, without hesitation, and yet without confusion, set fire to the several trains. In an instant, and with an explosion that shook the city and was distinctly heard at Meerut, the Magazine blew up. The wall was thrown flat upon the ground, and it was said that some hundreds of the enemy were buried under the ruins or blown into the air. Strange to say, half of that gallant band remained alive from amidst the ruins, blackened, singed, and wounded, but that they escaped at all cannot be more a matter of surprise to others than it is to themselves.

There was now no option for the British in Delhi but to pull out as soon as possible. By nightfall on 11 May the last Europeans had either scrambled from the city or been hunted down. The mutineers had achieved swift and staggering success, and even the attempted destruction of the magazine had left them 3,000 barrels of gunpowder intact. Moreover, their capture of Delhi had enormous symbolic significance, for in the dark recesses of the palace lived Bahadur Shah II, the last Mogul Emperor. Although a pensioner of the British, and an Emperor without an Empire, the mutineers exalted the reluctant old man to the former glories of his dynasty. With the Mogul Emperor restored at Delhi, and with news of the mutineers' triumph spreading like wildfire through the cantonments of the Ganges valley, there seemed little prospect of a prompt British recovery.

8
'Remember Cawnpore!'

As the British survivors from Delhi, together with European reinforcements, regrouped themselves on the ridge overlooking the city, the mutineers seemed victorious on all sides. Regiment after mutinous regiment poured into Delhi, their colours flying, weapons gleaming, their military bands playing British marching tunes. On Delhi Ridge there was chaos: for weeks nobody was able to assert command and organize for defence or attack. But in the middle of August John Nicholson, black-bearded, immense and resolute, marched in from the Punjab at the head of vital reinforcements; more fresh troops slowly trickled in. The mutineers within the great walls of Delhi grew uneasy; the fateful 17 June, the centenary of Clive's victory at Plassey, had come and gone without the predicted complete collapse of British rule. On 4 September a siege-train arrived with enough fire-power to grind Delhi to dust. By 21 September the city was captured, and the British were busy wreaking a bloody and often summary vengeance upon the defeated mutineers.

But while Delhi was in the hands of the rebel sepoys, the East India Company was reeling from a whole series of grievous blows elsewhere. The most savage of these fell in the disaffected province of Oudh. The Company's military headquarters in the province lay at Cawnpore. The need to provide reliable garrisons in the recently annexed territories of Sind and the Punjab had stripped Oudh of European troops, leaving only the 32nd Foot at Lucknow and a battery of the Bengal artillery. Even these scanty numbers were reduced when, after the fall of Delhi, the Commissioner for Oudh, Sir Henry Lawrence, took the majority under his own command.

Major-General Wheeler, an old man of fifty-four years' service, was the Company's commander in Oudh. He tried, somewhat ineffectually, to prepare Cawnpore against any impending rising. He was not successful, and Captain Fletcher Hayes, one of Sir Henry Lawrence's aides, wrote a gloomy description of the confusion that gripped Cawnpore:

> At six am I went out to have a look at the various places, and since I have been in India never witnessed so frightful a scene of confusion, fright, and bad arrangement as the European barracks presented. Four guns were in position loaded, with European artillery-men in nightcaps and wide-awakes and side-arms on, hanging to the guns in groups – looking like melodramatic buccaneers. People of all kinds, of every colour, sect and profession, were crowding into the barracks. While I was there, buggies ... vehicles of all sorts, drove up and discharged cargoes of writers, tradesmen, and a miscellaneous mob of every complexion, from white to tawny – all in terror of the imaginary foe; ladies sitting down at the rough mess-tables in the barracks, women suckling infants, ayahs and children in all directions, and – officers too! In short, as I have written to Sir Henry, I saw quite enough to convince me that if any insurrection took or takes place, we shall have no-one to thank but ourselves, because we have now shown the natives how very easily we can become frightened, and when frightened utterly helpless. During

that day (22 May) the shops in all the bazaars were shut, four or five times, and all the day the General was worried to death by people running up to report improbable stories, which in ten minutes more were contradicted by others still more monstrous. All yesterday (23rd) the same thing went on; and I wish that you could see the European barracks and the chapel close to it – and their occupants. I believe that if anything will keep the sepoys quiet, it will be, next to Providence, the great respect which they all have for General Wheeler, and for him alone. He has all his doors and windows open all night, and has never thought of moving or of allowing his family to move. Brigadier Jack, Parker the cantonment magistrate, and Wiggins, the Judge Advocate-General, are, I believe, the only people who sleep in their houses.

Still, May ended with Cawnpore and Lucknow still in British hands. Elsewhere the Company had not been so fortunate : there had been mutinous outbreaks at Aligarh, Bareilly, Bombay, Ferozepore and other smaller stations; sepoy regiments had been disarmed at Agra, Lahore, Mardan and Peshawar. It was still possible that the mutiny could be contained; apart from the capture of Delhi the rebels had no other spectacular success with which to dazzle their wavering comrades; a considerable number of sepoy regiments in the Bengal Army, moreover, continued to be loyal, and some even clamoured to be sent to Delhi to help crush the mutineers.

But on 24 May Colonel (later General) Neill, commanding the Madras Fusiliers, landed at Calcutta. Neill was soon to earn a fearsome reputation as the most vindictive of retributionists. His ruthless and barbarous conduct was the dark reflection of a psychopathic personality. Even before he had found the opportunity to exhibit his sadistic and homicidal tendencies, he helped to seal the fate of both Cawnpore and Lucknow. On 3 July he arrived at Benares, the sacred Hindu city on the Ganges. There he stubbornly insisted on disarming the sepoys in the garrison, but only after the situation had been grossly mishandled and passions inflamed.

From Benares, Neill pushed his men on to Allahabad along the Grand Trunk Road. Allahabad stood at the junction of the Ganges and Jumna rivers, and was of vital strategic importance to the control of the provinces of Oudh and Rohilkhand. Until 4 June the sepoys at Allahabad had been passive enough, which was just as well since there was no British garrison there. Then news of Neill's disarming of the troops at Benares reached Allahabad and within two days the 6th Native Infantry had mutinied, killing any Europeans that fell into their hands, and initiating an orgy of looting and arson. Fortunately most of the European civilian population had already taken refuge in the fort.

More than a month later, on 11 July, Neill reached Allahabad and began to wreak revenge on the mutineers. But in the intervening period the revolt at Allahabad had infected the territory to the north, making it almost impossible to move reinforcements into Oudh. All this contributed handsomely to the fall of Cawnpore and the siege of the Residency at Lucknow.

At Cawnpore as May drew to a close, General Wheeler, conscious that the sepoys there were on the brink of mutiny, twisted and turned to avoid antagonizing them. He refused, for this reason, to take over the magazine and turn it into a refuge for the European community – General Neill was later strongly critical of this decision, arguing that the magazine had 'a walled defence, walled enclosure, proof against musketry, covering an area of three acres, ample room for all the garrison, close to the bank of the river. . . . They could have moved out and attacked (the rebels) with their guns and would have not only saved themselves but the city, to say nothing of a large arsenal and many thousand stands of arms, artillery, tents, harness, etc. . .'

But at the end of May Neill was just striking out from Calcutta, and had yet to hang his first Muslim sepoy in a defiling pig skin. It was Wheeler who took the agonizing and, as it proved, catastrophic decision to abandon the magazine and instead fortify two military barracks at the eastern end of the European cantonment. Although the barracks were close to the river, they were defended only by a parapet of loose earth which was not even bullet-proof. Adequate provisions were not provided, and the one well from which the defenders could draw water was out in the open and within range of the enemy's guns.

Wheeler's belief that he could contain his sepoys by not provoking them, was at first justified by events. But it was, in fact, a gamble with the lives of the tiny European garrison of 240 soldiers and 375 women and children. The wife of one of the senior garrison officers, Colonel Ewart, saw the terrible dangers of the tense situation:

> Our weak positions here, with a mere handful of Europeans, places us in very great danger; and daily and hourly we are looking for disasters. It is supposed that the commandants here have shown wonderful tact, that their measure of boldly facing the danger by going out to sleep amongst their men has had a wonderful effect in restraining them. But everybody knows that this cannot last. Any accidental spark may set the whole of the regiments of infantry, and one of cavalry, in a blaze of mutiny.

The outbreak came at last on the night of 4 June when the 2nd Native Cavalry and the 1st Native Infantry mutinied and marched off to ransack the Cawnpore treasury which was situated in the suburb of Nawabganji on the road to Bithur. Ominous though this rebellion was, it still fell far short of disaster for the tiny European community in Cawnpore: the 53rd and 56th Native Infantry regiments were apparently anxious to prove their loyalty, and the mutinous sepoy units had refrained from attacking their officers. Moreover, at Bithur resided the Maharaja, Nana Sahib, who had on 22 May sent two guns and three hundred troops to reinforce General Wheeler. These men Wheeler promptly stationed near the magazine and the treasury.

But the British position at Cawnpore was, in fact, about to collapse. Wheeler must bear much of the blame for this, for on the morning of 5 June, convinced that a further mutiny was imminent, he turned his guns on the lines of the 53rd Infantry as they were cooking their breakfasts. The outraged 53rd mutinied on the spot, as did a considerable number of the 56th – though all their Indian officers and many of the men loyally insisted on joining the British within their entrenchments.

Even so, all was not lost, for the disaffected men of the 53rd and the 56th Native Infantry did not turn on their erstwhile masters, but marched off towards Delhi – still the great citadel of the mutineers, and the most potent symbol of their success. But, tragically for the British garrison at Cawnpore, the rebel detachments never reached Delhi. On 6 June Wheeler received a letter from the Maharaja of Bithur, Nana Sahib, informing him that he was about to be attacked. When a few hours later guns opened fire on the Cawnpore entrenchments, they were, almost unbelievably, Nana Sahib's guns.

What had transformed the cooperative prince of 22 May into the vindictive adversary of 6 June? To be sure, Nana Sahib had his grievances: he was the eldest adopted son of the last King of the once mighty Maratha dynasty; but on his adoptive father's death the administration of Lord Dalhousie had abolished the Maratha title and the annual pension of £8,000 which Nana Sahib should have inherited. Though remaining Maharaja of Bithur, Nana found himself in financial difficulties by 1857. Yet he was on good terms with the British commanders and administrators at Cawnpore, and was by no means fanatically committed to his religion.

But between 5 and 6 June Nana Sahib decided to lead his own troops and the Cawnpore mutineers against General Wheeler. Harbouring resentments, struggling with his debts, Nana probably believed that the days of British rule were over, and that he could profit from hastening the ruin of the East India Company. It is also likely that the mutinous troops put tremendous pressure on him to lead them in an assault on Cawnpore.

Whatever the true story, from 6 to 25 June Nana's guns pounded the British entrenchments under an implacable, broiling sun. The defects of Wheeler's disposition of his troops was now all too horribly evident, even to one of the besieged, the eighteen-year-old Amelia Home:

> It was one of the most terrible sights which our eyes now beheld; the whole surrounding country seemed covered with men at arms, on horse and on foot, and they presented a most formidable appearance. They seemed such odds to keep at bay from our Lilliputian defences.
>
> The site of our entrenchment was surrounded by large and substantial buildings, from three to eight hundred yards distance, occupied by the rebels, and from roof and window, all day, a shower of bullets poured down upon us in our exposed position. Shells likewise kept falling all over the entrenchment, and every shot that struck the barracks was followed by the heart-rending shrieks of the women and children, who were either killed outright by the projectiles, or crushed to death by the falling beams, masonry, and splinters. One shell killed seven women as it fell hissing into the trenches and burst. Windows and doors were soon shot off their sockets, and the shot and shell began to play freely through the denuded buildings. . . .
>
> At first we briskly replied to the fire, but without much effect. Our guns were too small, nor was it thought advisable to exhaust our small store of ammunition, as the rebels took good care to keep well under cover.

Despite the occasional heroic sortie, and the constant hope that reinforcements would somehow reach them, the garrison at Cawnpore were caught like rats in a trap. The outposts of the entrenchment could only be supplied with ammunition by volunteers running a gauntlet of fire from the besiegers; the mutineers' guns set alight the thatched hospital barracks; food supplies dwindled so alarmingly that the remaining sepoys were dismissed with a certificate of loyalty.

Nobody was safe, as the following eyewitness account shows:

There was a room safer, comparatively speaking, than the rest, and one night two little girls, about eight or nine years old, were left in it by their parents, whose agony it is impossible to describe when they returned the following morning and found that a shell had burst in the room and killed them. They were simply torn to pieces, bones, brains, and flesh strewn all over, and not a step could you take without treading on some portion of their remains. These were reverently collected together in a sheet and thrown into the well.

By 25 June the depleted garrison was in a desperate state. Amelia Home described the occupants as:

Worked to death; underfed, and, in the later stages of the siege, starved; continually under a hot fire from the mutiners; their uniforms rotting on their backs; their faces unwashed; their hands covered with grime from the guns, which dried and formed a hard coating; they were such a pitiful sight to see. Our artillerymen, one by one, dropped at their guns, and were replaced by volunteers from the civilians, who had to be trained to their new, unfamiliar, and nerve-trying duties. . . . Great difficulty was experienced in the removal of the dead. . . . They were piled in a corner of the verandah, kept there until late at night, when the fire abating, they were consigned to the well. The stench from our room was insufferable, and our suffering from want of water I cannot describe. . . . There was a clergyman amongst us who died raving mad through the combined effects of heat, exposure, and fear, and used to walk about stark naked. His condition was pitiable to see.

Unfortunately even the vision of a naked clergyman could not keep the mutineers at bay. Wheeler's forces could hold out no longer, and on 26 June a truce was declared under which the British would surrender their artillery and treasure, and evacuate the entrenchments; in return the troops could keep their hand-arms and 60 rounds of ammunition, and Nana undertook to provide river transport for the women and children, the sick and the wounded.

On 27 June the British survivors marched towards the Sati Chandra Ghat on the Ganges river. No sooner were most of the civilians and wounded loaded on to the boats than a terrible and bloody massacre ensued; the thatched roofs of some boats were set on fire by the mutineers, and a volley of musket fire crashed into the panic-stricken passengers. Amelia Home, who survived the slaughter, left an agonizing account of the tragedy:

> While we were endeavouring to embark the shore was lined with spectators. . . . After all had embarked – which took about two hours to accomplish – the word was given to proceed. Instead of the crews obeying the order, a signal was given from the shore, and they all leaped into the water and waded to the bank, after having first secreted burning charcoal in the thatch of most of the boats. Immediately a volley of bullets assailed us, followed by a hail of shot and grape. The two soldiers seated alongside of me were wounded, and crept into the shelter of the awning to escape being made further targets of. In a few minutes pandemonium reigned. The boats were seen to be wrapped in flames, and the wounded were burnt to death. Some jumped overboard and tried to swim to the opposite shore, but were picked off by the bullets of the sepoys. Others were drowned, while a few others jumped into the water and hid behind their boats to escape the pitiless fire. But the guns continued their vile work, and grape and musketry were poured into the last-mentioned people from the opposite bank which soon became alive with rebels, placed there to intercept refugees to that shore. A few succeeded in pushing their boats to the further side of the river and were mercilessly slaughtered.
>
> The cavalry waded into the river with drawn swords and cut down those who were still alive, while the infantry boarded the boats to loot. One unfortunate, a Mr Kirkpatrick, in trying to ward off the blows from a sabre with

his arms, had both arms chopped off. I saw him about half an hour later lying in the water still alive!

The air resounded with the shrieks of the women and children, and agonized prayers to God for mercy. The water was red with blood, and the smoke from the heavy firing of the cannon and muskets and the fire from the burning boats lay like dense clouds all around us. Several men were multilated in the presence of their wives, while babes and children were torn from their mother's arms and hacked to pieces.

One boat did get away, but only four of its passengers survived. Of those British who were not killed during the massacre at the Ghat, 60 soldiers were later wiped out by the Nana's troops, and the women and children imprisoned in a small house near the abandoned entrenchments. On 15 July the final horrible act of the dramatic fall of Cawnpore occurred when, on hearing that a relieving force under General Havelock was approaching the city, the mutineers murdered the remaining women and children and cast their mutilated bodies down a well.

The massacres at Cawnpore were only part of the dark and savage deeds that were commonplace during the Mutiny. Doubtless the rebels were encouraged in their ruthless behaviour by the terrifying whirlwind of British revenge that was already sweeping through Oudh. Before Havelock's men reached Cawnpore, General Neill had sent ahead a small detachment of 820 European and loyal Indian troops under Major Renaud. As Havelock's forces (numbering 1000 European soldiers and 130 Sikhs) followed Renaud's path they saw stark evidence of retribution:

In the first two days of our march towards Cawnpore we passed several dead bodies hanging from trees by the roadside. These had been executed by Renaud's men, presumably for complicity in the mutiny; but I am afraid some innocent men suffered; a comrade who ought to know said that 'Renaud was rather inclined to hang all black creation'. In every case, where the feet were near the ground, pigs (either wild or belonging to the villagers) had eaten the lower parts of the bodies; the stench from the latter, in the moist still air, was intolerable.

On 17 July Havelock's forces attacked Cawnpore and drove Nana Sahib's men out. Nana escaped with his family, and evaded capture, probably dying in Nepal in 1859. Less fortunate were the mutineers who fell into General Neill's hands when Havelock pushed on towards Lucknow on 25 July. Rumours of Neill's violent retributions had already contributed to dogged sepoy resistance, and possibly to the Cawnpore massacres. His reaction to the horrors that he found there provides a grisly evidence of his idea of proper retribution :

Whenever a rebel is caught he is immediately tried, and unless he can prove a defence he is sentenced to be hanged at once; but the chief rebels or ringleaders I make clean up a certain portion of the pool of blood, still two inches deep [sic!] in the shed where the fearful murder and mutilation of women and children took place.

To touch blood is most abhorrent to the high-caste natives, they think that by doing so they doom their souls to perdition. Let them think so. My object is to inflict a most fearful punishment for a revolting, cowardly, barbarous deed, and to strike terror into these rebels.

The first I caught was a subadhar, a native officer, a high-caste Brahmin, who tried to resist my order to clean up the very blood he had helped to shed; but I made the Provost-Marshal do his duty, and a few lashes soon made the miscreant accomplish his task. Which done, he was taken out and immediately hanged, and after death buried in a ditch at the roadside.

No one who has witnessed the scenes of murder, mutilation, and massacre can ever listen to the word 'mercy' as applied to these fiends. The well of mutilated bodies – containing upwards of 200 women and children – I have had decently covered in and built up as one large grave.

9
The Siege of Lucknow

While Cawnpore had been caught in the torment of mutiny, Lucknow, forty-eight miles away, underwent a similar, though less successful, rebellion. Here Sir Henry Lawrence, Chief Commissioner for Oudh, assumed the rank of Brigadier on hearing, between 14 and 15 May, of the mutiny at Meerut and the fall of Delhi. Lawrence soon showed the advantages of resolute leadership, combined with tact. A Swiss-born wholesale merchant, L.E. Routz Rees, was full of praise for the Chief Commissioner:

> Sir Henry Lawrence was indefatigable, and seemed almost never to sleep. Often would he sally out in disguise, and visit the most frequented parts of the native town, to make personal observations, and see how his orders were carried out. He several times had a thin bedding spread out near the guns at the Bailey-guard Gate, and retired there among the artillerists, not to sleep, but to plan and meditate undisturbed. He appeared to be ubiquitous.

Lawrence also attempted to understand sepoy grievances and to allay them where possible; this undoubtedly accounted for the sizeable minority of Indian loyalists at Lucknow. At the same time he ordered a pentagonal entrenchment to be thrown up around the Residency. Compared with the cramped and vulnerable entrenchment at Cawnpore, the Residency site offered its defenders a very fair chance of a successful resistance. The main criticism of Lawrence's activities at this time was that, anxious to avoid offending Indian feelings, he failed to order the destruction of mosques and temples on the edge of the entrenchments, thus affording excellent positions for rebel snipers later on.

On 30 May there was a brief eruption, when many of the sepoys rose in revolt. Lawrence, however, managed to rally the men of the 32nd Foot, and the insurgents fled. The next day Lawrence pursued them for ten miles and brought back sixty prisoners. But the news of the Lucknow mutiny inspired similar revolts at Bareilly and Shahjahanpur to the north-west on 31 May. Between 3 and 6 June mutinies broke out to the south and east at Azamgarh, Benares, Jaunpur, Cawnpore and Allahabad. On 3 June the 41st Native Infantry rebelled at Sitapur to the west, and on 8 June Faizabad, then Sultanpur, also fell.

Despite this wholesale collapse of British power on every side, Lawrence doggedly continued with the fortification of the Lucknow Residency. Towards the end of June the garrison heard of General Wheeler's capitulation at Cawnpore. On 28 June Lawrence moved both troops and civilians into the Residency entrenchment. He was then persuaded into undertaking an aggressive foray against the mutineers closing in around Lucknow. This move resulted in a sharp defeat for the British forces, and contributed a good deal to the subsequent trials during the siege of the Residency.

On 29 June the advancing mutineers were reported at Chinhut, about ten miles from Lucknow. Believing that there were less than 600 sepoys at Chinhut, and under pressure to teach the rebels a rousing lesson, Lawrence marched against them. This was itself an ill-considered move, and was rendered more hazardous by Lawrence's assumption of the command of the expedition despite his own lack of military experience. The force consisted of 300 men of the 32nd Foot, 170 sepoys of the 13th Native Infantry, 100 Sikhs of the Oudh Irregular Cavalry, 35 troopers of the Volunteer Horse, Indian gunners with ten field pieces, and a howitzer drawn by elephants.

Seven miles from Chinhut, Lawrence, having encountered no rebels, was on the point of returning to Lucknow, when he received the completely erronous information that Chinhut contained no enemy forces – and changed his mind. The direct result of this decision was a small-scale, but highly significant, disaster for British arms. For at Chinhut were waiting over six thousand mutineers, with some sixteen guns. Lawrence's men were tired and hungry (the 32nd had unaccountably brought no food with them) and were beginning to wilt under the blazing summer sun.

The mutineers were well positioned and led by a commander indisputably more able than Lawrence. The Indian artillerymen deserted Lawrence; the 32nd Queen's Foot were shot to pieces, only three officers and 116 men surviving, Lawrence himself belatedly handed over command to Colonel Inglis and returned post-haste to Lucknow to prepare the Residency against imminent attack. As the battered and defeated troops followed Lawrence into Lucknow the enemy's roundshot whistled about their ears.

That night Lawrence put the position frankly in an urgent letter to General Havelock :

> This morning we went out to Chinhut to meet the enemy, and we were defeated, and lost five guns through the misconduct of our native artillery, many of whom deserted. The enemy have followed us up, and we have now been besieged for four hours, and shall probably tonight be surrounded. The enemy are very bold, some Europeans very low. I look on our position now as ten times as bad as it was yesterday; indeed it is very critical. We shall have to abandon much supplies and to blow up

much powder. Unless we are relieved quickly, say in fifteen or twenty days, we shall hardly be able to maintain our position. We lost three officers killed this morning and several wounded.

In the eyes of the Swiss merchant Routz Rees confusion had gripped Lucknow:

> The enemy now at our door, as it were, the crowded streets began to be entirely deserted. People were flying in all directions up the streets as far away from the Residency as possible. Horses without riders galloped up and down; elephants and camels were hurried away by their drivers; and the boats on the river shoved off far away from the English encampment and the iron bridge. Soon not a living man was seen. All outside our entrenchments was as quiet and still as if it were a city of the dead.

Although the defenders of Lucknow had a better chance of holding out than had the garrison at Cawnpore, they faced appalling difficulties. There were only 1,600 fighting men out of the 3,100 within the entrenchment; rebel snipers were soon firing at will from the mosques that Lawrence had refused to demolish; food supplies were limited; the enemy's morale and prestige had been boosted tremendously by their victory at Chinhut. On 2 July a further heavy blow fell when Lawrence suffered a fatal wound from an exploding shell, and the command was divided between a civil and a military officer.

By 29 July, however, forces under Generals Havelock and Neill had defeated Nana Sahib at Cawnpore and advanced to within two miles of Lucknow. At this point Havelock prudently decided to fall back and regroup his disease-stricken and badly mauled force. Badgered and insulted by Neill, who favoured pressing on to Lucknow, Havelock threatened his belligerent second-in-command with arrest, Still, he felt unable to relieve Lucknow without substantial reinforcements – not surprisingly in view of the 30,000 mutineers besieging the Residency.

Despite the deprivations and suffering of the Lucknow garri-

son, it was not until 27 September that a force of some 3,000
British troops led jointly by Generals Outram (who was in fact
the new commander) and Havelock fought their way into the
Residency. But even this triumph was short-lived; nearly a third
of the attacking army had been killed or wounded (among the
former being the bloodthirsty General Neill who was shot through
the head as he entered the Residency); Havelock and Outram
could not break out, and found themselves in turn besieged.
Fortunately one of the relieving forces discovered two months'
supplies that had been laid down by Lawrence unbeknown to his
commissariat officers!

The second siege of Lucknow ended on 17 November 1857,
when 5,000 men stormed through to the Residency led by the
vigorous and forthright Sir Colin Campbell, the newly appointed
Commander-in-Chief in India. Campbell had earlier won fame
for his sterling work at the Battle of Alma in the Crimean War
where he had commanded the Highland Brigade. Now, as at the
Alma, Scottish troops of the 93rd Highland Regiment, together
with Sikhs, Punjabis and English infantrymen, played a conspicuous part in the gory assault.

But even though the Residency was relieved, and hundreds of
mutineers shot and hacked to pieces by the relieving troops,
Lucknow itself remained in enemy hands. Campbell withdrew to
deal with a fresh threat to Cawnpore, leaving Outram in charge
at Lucknow (where on 24 November Havelock, having achieved
acclaim as a God-fearing avenger of unspeakable wrongs, died of
dysentery). It was not until 15 March 1858 that the city of
Lucknow was reconquered by the British. In the interim, however, thousands of mutineers had escaped, and many had joined
with rebel forces in Central India, where the Rani of Jhansi had
abandoned her womanly deportment and was waging a successful
campaign against an army led by Sir Hugh Rose.

With Lucknow recaptured, however, the core was knocked out
of the mutineers' position in Oudh. Other enemy strongholds fell
throughout 1858: Jhansi, Bareilly, Jagdispur and Gwalior.
Between July and December 1858 rebel bands were suppressed in

all regions except Rajputana and Central India where Tantia Topi, the erstwhile lieutenant of Nana Sahib, kept up a guerilla campaign. But in April 1859 Tantia Topi was betrayed and executed.

Thus ended the great Indian Mutiny, after gorging the Victorian imagination on unprecedented horrors and on lofty examples of self-sacrifice, fortitude and gallantry. In 1858 the Crown assumed the administrative functions of the East India Company, the Governor-General became the Viceroy, and a Secretary of State for India was created in London. Between rulers and ruled the gulf that had long existed now seemed permanent and quite impassable. British rule in the sub-continent seemed firmer than ever, and rested on the bayonets of a far greater proportion of European troops (about one third) than before the Mutiny.

Yet in military terms it had been, as the Duke of Wellington observed, on a previous occasion, 'a damned close-run thing'. Despite the lack of any consistent or coherent plan among the mutineers, the British forces had only with difficulty destroyed the uprising. The vastly superior strength of the rebel forces had accounted for many early reverses, but this is not a sufficient explanation; nor is the susceptibility of European troops to disease, though 8,987 perished in this way as opposed to the 2,034 who died as a result of enemy action.

The plain truth is that the campaign to contain and suppress the Mutiny was characterized by military incompetence from first to last. On the whole the commanders exhibited fatal indecision and frequently lacked resolution. Rancour between 'Queen's men' and 'Company men', as exemplified by the quarrels of Havelock and Neill, was a disruptive influence. There was appalling organization, and, all too commonly, an over-heated appraisal of the facts. If the Mutiny was merely a transient intoxication for rebels in north and central India, it provided a near fatal draught for an encumbered and inefficient military leadership.

Part IV
The Zulu War 1879

I do kill; but do not consider that I have done anything
yet in the way of killing. . . . I have not yet begun; I have
yet to kill; it is the custom of our nation and I shall not
depart from it.

Cetshwayo, King of the Zulus, to the
Governor of Natal, Sir Henry Bulwer, 1878

The Zulus are more dangerous than you think. It
was because we Boers held them too cheaply that we
sustained such loss.

J. J. Uys to Lord Chelmsford before the
invasion of Zululand in January 1879

10
The Invasion is Launched

The Zulu war of 1879 derived directly from the British annexations of the Afrikaner republic of the Transvaal in 1877. There was one overriding reason why the government of the fiercely independent Boers of the Transvaal had grudgingly accepted British rule in 1877 : they believed that the stability of their impoverished province would be assured. British funds and investments would flow in, and the troublesome Bantu tribes on the borders would be pacified by the exercise of Imperial might. The majority of Transvaalers, however, resented the annexation to which President Burgers had assented, and found their spokesman in their able and unyielding Vice-President Paul Kruger.

The need to temper the opposition of the high veld Boers became essential for British policymakers, for whom the annexation promised a neat north-eastern confederation between Natal, Griqualand West and the Transvaal. With the Cape a self-governing British colony, and the Boer republic of the Orange Free State dependent upon its neighbours for trade and, ultimately, defence, British influence would prevail from the Limpopo to Cape Town. All of southern Africa could then be led towards a federation beneath the Union Jack.

But before the European settlers and traders, both Boer and British, could begin to exploit their environment to the full it was desirable to pacify the local African tribes. Throughout southern Africa a variety of African peoples competed for living space and cattle: Fingoes, Basutos, Swazis, Gcalekas, Xhosas and many more. Most of these tribes belonged to the Bantu people who had drifted southwards, at the same speed as their driven herds of cattle, during the eighteenth century. Of all the Bantu tribes the Zulu became the most warlike and formidable.

By 1877 the Zulus had established their paramountcy over territory to the north-east of the British colony of Natal; Zululand stretched from the banks of the Tugela river to Portuguese Mozambique in the north; it shared a hundred-mile frontier with Natal and one of more than one hundred and twenty miles with the Transvaal. Under great warrior chieftains like Shaka and Dingane the Zulu nation had been moulded into a well-disciplined and highly effective military machine. Though after Dingane's rule Mpande had allowed a deterioration in Zulu military organization, his successor, Cetshwayo, decided to re-establish the martial traditions of the legendary Shaka.

Cetshwayo had begun his eventful reign in 1873 when he established himself as master in the royal Kraal at Ulundi. Nearly 50,000 Zulu males were under arms, of which more than 40,000 were less than sixty years of age and organized into twenty-six corps. The Zulu regiments, or impis, accepted an enforced celibacy until they had exhibited prowess in battle; once this 'washing of the spears' had been accomplished the chief accorded them iKhela status and they were free to marry.

The existence of this huge army so close to European settlements in Natal and the Transvaal was bound to cause consistent tension. The Afrikaners of the Transvaal in particular had no love for the Bantu and were quite prepared to defend their frontiers by whatever means lay at hand. When the British agent

Theophilus Shepstone had pushed through the annexation of the Transvaal he had managed to avert an impending conflict with the Zulu nation. If continuing Afrikaner acquiescence in their subordinate status had to be bought, then perhaps the price was a general pacification of south-eastern Africa at the expense of the Zulus.

The need to tame the belligerent impis of Cetshwayo and to placate the high veld Boers was also recognized by the newly-appointed Governor of the Cape and High Commissioner for South Africa, Sir Bartle Frere. Soon after he took up his office in 1877 Frere became convinced that the Zulus must be broken, as the first, and major, step in the federating of southern Africa. Two incidents provided excellent justification for his attitude.

The first occurred when Cetshwayo granted two regiments of early middle-aged warriors the right to marry after they had undertaken a successful punitive expedition. He directed them, however, to take their wives from a much younger group of females called the inGcugce. Most of these girls already considered themselves betrothed to youths in other regiments. After much confusion Cetshwayo proclaimed that an inGcugce found living with a man under forty years old was to be executed and her father's cattle seized. About half a dozen girls were actually killed before the majority either accepted elderly husbands or fled into Natal or the Transvaal. Some were caught as they tried to escape and their bodies adorned the main tracks from Zululand as a fearsome deterrent.

In July 1878 a further bloody episode took place. Two unfaithful wives of the Zulu induna Sihayo crossed the border into Natal to escape vengeance. Pursuing warriors forded the Tugela river and tracked down the adulterous women, who they then dragged back to Zulu territory and executed. Though justified in Zulu law, these killings brought a protest from the British authorities in Natal whose indignation was perhaps increased by the fact that one errant wife had been caught and executed by her own son.

Cetshwayo was in no mood to accept British protests meekly. Though merciful by the standards of his forbears, he was, to

European eyes, a blood-stained tyrant. When reminded that at his coronation he had been advised by Shepstone to avoid indiscriminate killings Cetshwayo replied in haughty and uncompromising terms to the Governor of Natal, Sir Henry Bulwer :

> Did I ever tell Shepstone I would not kill? Did he tell the white people I made such an arrangement? Because if he did so he deceived them. I do kill; but do not consider that I have done anything yet in the way of killing. Why do the white people start at nothing? I have not yet begun; I have yet to kill; it is the custom of our nation and I shall not depart from it. Why does the Governor of Natal speak to me about my laws? Do I go to Natal and dictate to him about his laws? I shall not agree to any laws or rules from Natal, and by doing so throw the large kraal which I govern into the water. My people will not listen unless they are killed; and while wishing to be friends with the English I do not agree to give my people over to be governed by laws sent to me by them. Have I not asked the English to allow me to wash my spears since the death of my father Mpande, and they have kept playing with me all this time, treating me like a child? Go back and tell the English that I shall now act on my own account, and if they wish me to agree to their laws, I shall leave and become a wanderer; but before I go it will be seen, as I shall not go without having acted. Go back and tell the white people this, and let them hear it well. The Governor of Natal and I are in like positions : he is Governor of Natal, and I am Governor here.

Bartle Frere made brisk use of Cetshwayo's proud reply, and of the incidents that had led to it, to convince his superiors in London that it was vital to break the Zulus once and for all. In October 1878 Frere wrote: 'I can only repeat my own conviction that the continued preservation of peace depends no longer on what the servants of the British Government here may do or abstain from doing, but simply on the caprice of an ignorant and bloodthirsty despot, with an organized force of at least 40,000 armed men at his absolute command.'

Unable to wring reinforcements out of London, Frere cajoled Bulwer, the Governor of Natal, into levying 7000 Natal Kaffirs to serve with the British forces should war break out with the Zulus. In December 1878 Theophilus Shepstone presided over a fateful meeting with Zulu leaders at the Lower Drift of the Tugela. The apparent object of the meeting was to present the findings of the Boundary Commission that had recently considered the rival claims of the Zulus and the Transvaalers to the Blood River territory. Though Frere had undoubtedly tampered with the report, Shepstone still had no choice but to announce the recognition of Zulu sovereignty over the territory; at the same time, however, Boer residential rights in the area were upheld, thus effectively denying Zulu sovereignty.

The assembled indunas and lesser chieftains now prepared to leave, but Shepstone made them a present of a bullock and asked them to return after eating it. When the indaba reassembled the Zulu chieftains listened with mounting indignation to a list of demands from Frere. Among the more provocative of these was the order to disband the Zulu army and to abandon the whole military system established by Shaka and his heirs. In addition, Shepstone's advice to Cetshwayo at his coronation regarding indiscriminate killing was to be obeyed, and the warriors who had pursued and executed the two unfaithful wives of chief Sihayo must be handed over for trial by the Natal courts. There were nine other demands. Some of the demands had to be met within three days, others within thirty; all were bound to antagonize Cetshwayo and strip him of much of his power.

In short, Frere had presented the Zulu nation with a complicated ultimatum that would inevitably be rejected. By doing so the High Commissioner had provoked a war, and in such a way that the British government would not learn that fighting had broken out until it was well under way. For their part the Zulu indunas who bore the news of Frere's ultimatum back to Ulundi were not unduly pessimistic at the prospect of war with the

British; they knew little of the fire-power of European armies, and were steeped in the history of their victorious tribal campaigns. But Cetshwayo was more anxious to avoid war, and actually agreed to several of Frere's demands. But the sticking point, of course, was the abandonment of the Zulu military system. This was quite impossible for Cetshwayo, and on 11 January 1879 Frere announced that British forces were crossing into Zululand 'to exact from Cetywayo reparations for violations of British territory committed by the sons of Sirayo and others; and to enforce compliance with the promises, made by Cetywayo at his coronation, for the better government of his people.' The announcement continued, somewhat optimistically in view of the events of the next few weeks. 'When the war is finished the British Government will make the best arrangements in its power for the future good government of the Zulus in their own country, in peace and quietness, and will not permit the killing and oppression they have suffered from Cetywayo to continue.'

Lord Chelmsford commanded the invasion of Zululand. He had 16,800 men, 2,000,000 rounds of ammunition, nearly 8,000 commissariat animals, and over 700 carts and wagons. Some 6,000 of the troops were British redcoats, drawn from the 3rd, 4th, 13th, 24th, 90th and 99th Foot Regiments; there were twenty nine-pounder field guns. Most of the officers and men had seen action before : in the Crimea, the Indian Mutiny, the Second Opium War, the invasion of Abyssinia and the Second Maori War. The foot soldiers wore cork sun helmets, red jackets, blue trousers and heavy iron-shod boots. They were thus not encapsuled in the gaudy and irrelevant finery that had characterized the British troops at the outbreak of the Crimean War; nonetheless, their uniforms were ill-suited to the scorching glare of the African sun.

The infantrymen carried the breech-loading 1871 Martini-Henry rifle, which fired a single heavy slug and recoiled violently. It also tended to over-heat if fired many times in succession. The men bore no other arms except the bayonet, but they staggered under the weight of various knapsacks, ammunition pouches and spare equipment, unless they could throw all but the most essential items into the campaign waggons that accompanied them. The men were resolute enough, and reckoned themselves well-fed by contemporary standards. They were fiercely loyal to their regiments, well-disciplined and sensible.

But there were barely 6,000 of them, and the Zulu warriors numbered more than 40,000. Nor did Lord Chelmsford possess a single squadron of regular British cavalry. However local volunteers provided a scratch cavalry force : there were 400 men of the Natal Mounted Police, 236 of Baker's Horse from Cape Colony and 216 troopers of the Frontier Light Horse. There were also forty mounted Afrikaners led and equipped by the redoubtable Piet Uys from the Blood River territory. All in all, there were over a thousand mounted volunteers at Lord Chelmsford's disposal, many of them with first-hand experience of the terrain. This at least meant that the invasion force would have enough 'eyes' as it marched into enemy territory, for the mounted men would carry out the essential tasks of scouting and reconnaissance. In addition there were over 7,000 Natal Kaffirs, recruited from the colony's native tribes and led by European officers and NCOs. They were a motley crew : their only approximation to uniform was a red rag tied round the head; most of them carried only rudimentary weapons like knobkerries and throwing assegais, though one in ten was equipped with a fire-arm of some sort. Unable to drill properly, and finding it difficult to understand the rough and often inadequate Zulu of their officers, the Natal Kaffirs presented a bizarre sight, provoking European observers to laughter rather than filling them with confidence. The invasion force also included several hundred African waggon drivers, pioneers, and servants, as well as some native cavalry.

Despite the defects in training and equipment of the Natal Kaffir regiments, the discipline and fire-power of the British battalions, backed by artillery, were sufficient to destroy the massed impis of Cetshwayo. The Zulu warriors were generally lacking in firearms, though a few possessed them; instead they relied at a distance upon the throwing assegai, and upon the short stabbing

H

assegai and the knobkerry for hand to hand fighting. Reliance on these weapons meant that they had to close with their enemy before being able to harm him. In this case, properly organized European troops could keep back the advancing warriors provided they could concentrate a rapid enough fire on the massed impis. The Zulus' oval cowhide shields could be pierced like tissue paper by the bullets from the Martini-Henry rifles.

Lord Chelmsford and his senior officers thus viewed the impending struggle with considerable confidence. Less satisfactory was the matter of supplying the army as it pushed into Zululand. The royal Kraal at Ulundi lay less than 75 miles from the point of invasion. It might possibly be reached in six weeks by the British forces, but this would have been good going. Even if it took only six weeks to sight Ulundi this would involve the transportation of something like 1,500 tons of rations, equipment and ammunition. The task of organizing the waggons, drivers and transport animals was an enormous one, and the problems and demands of the Transport Service multiplied so fast that they threatened to swamp other necessary activities. By scouring Natal for the appropriate animals and waggons, Chelmsford eventually assembled sufficient transport by the beginning of January 1879. Even so the invading columns could only travel as fast as their supply waggons, and these were liable to get stuck in drifts (river crossings) or to smash their wheels on boulders. Half a century ago the world had entered the Age of Steam, but the columns invading Zululand were able to march no quicker than Caesar's legions so many centuries before.

Still, Chelmsford and his officers had done their best to organize an effective supply system. Far more disturbing was the commander's decision to send three invasion columns against the Zulu impis. Not only did this mean that there was the danger of a breakdown of communication between the separated forces, but also that an already heavily-outnumbered army was split into three much smaller groups. If any of the British columns were to run into, say, half of the Zulu forces they would be hard pressed to hold their own.

As the British and Kaffir regiments moved off to the assembly points along the Tugela river, however, the prospect of annihilation seemed far removed. The troops marched out of Pietermaritzburg, Durban and Greytown, their bands playing tunes like 'I'm Leaving Thee in Sorrow, Annie'. Bishop Colenso, who believed the war to be unjust, gave them his guarded blessing. But as the redcoated battalions stepped it out, as the Natal Hussars and the Frontier Light Horse clattered off, and as Piet Uys rode down with his burghers, the British army was less than three weeks away from humiliation and disaster.

Lord Chelmsford's hopes, however, were high despite the grim advice given him by J.J. Uys, the brother of Piet Uys:

On January 6th [two weeks before the battle of Isandhlwana] I went with my son to ride to my brother Piet for the purpose of seeing him in the camp with Colonel Wood on the other side of Blood River, and on the way called again to see Lord Chelmsford in camp at Rorke's Drift. The general was very kind to us. We breakfasted with him, and he offered us an escort to Colonel Wood's camp at Kambula, but I told him I did not consider it necessary, that I was acquainted with the country and the Zulus, and would manage to get through all right. I said to the general, 'Be on your guard and be very careful. I have knowledge of the deceit and treachery of the Zulu nation. Trek into Zululand with two laagers close together. Place your spies far out and form your wagons into a round laager. The Zulus are more dangerous than you think. It was because we Boers held them too cheaply that we sustained such loss. Afterwards when we went with Andries Pretorius we were more careful to have our wagons closed well up. We sent our spies far out, and in this way we managed to beat the Zulus.'

11
The Invasion is Repulsed

On 11 January 1879 the three invasion forces began to move off. Lord Chelmsford led the centre column, which crossed the Tugela at Rorke's Drift and marched towards Ulundi by way of Isandhlwana mountain. The northern column, under General Evelyn Wood, forded Blood River and advanced towards Kambula and Hlobane. In the south, a column commanded by Colonel Charles Pearson pressed into Zululand over the Lower Drift of the Tugela. Chelmsford's three-pronged assault was in fact an eerie replica of the current Zulu strategy of attacking their enemy in three columns: the Right Horn, the Left Horn, and the Chest (the centre). Despite the implied compliment of imitation, the British assault columns were doomed to failure, while the Chest commanded by Lord Chelmsford himself was about to stumble into a disastrous defeat.

By 22 January the centre invasion force had established a staging camp below Isandhlwana mountain. Early that morning Lord Chelmsford took out part of the force on reconnaissance, leaving Colonel Pulleine in charge of the camp. Pulleine had 600 men of the 24th Regiment of Foot, as well as troopers of the Colonial Horse, artillery, and African auxiliaries. Moreover Colonel Durnford was approaching from Rorke's Drift with the reserve.

When Durnford reached the camp, however, Colonel Pulleine had become aware that there were a number of Zulus near the camp, though as yet nobody knew how many. Soon reports from scouts caused Durnford to come to the conclusion that the rear of Chelmsford's reconnoitring force was in danger. Accordingly he set off with the reserves to follow the Zulu warriors along the Nqutu Plateau. Captain George Shepstone (one of Theophilius Shepstone's six sons) was sent off with his native cavalry to track down the Zulus; one of these men cantered after some Zulu herdsmen over the lip of a ravine on the Nqutu Plateau. There to his amazement he saw thousands of Zulu warriors sitting tightly packed and silent on the floor of the ravine. They stretched as far as the eye could see. Numbering more than 20,000, they represented half of Cetshwayo's forces. Five days previously they had set out from Ulundi and had managed to evade detection, and Lord Chelmsford's reconnaissance, until now.

The solitary trooper turned and galloped frantically back to warn his companions. Simultaneously the Zulu host clambered to its feet and began to climb out of the ravine. The first that George Shepstone knew of the dire peril in which he and his comrades were placed was when he saw the astounding sight of the massed impis, stretched over a mile from wing to wing, trotting towards him. Shepstone raced back to the camp to warn Pulleine of the impending attack. Pulleine made a hasty disposition of three companies of the 24th Regiment to guard the north-east of the camp. He also sent Chelmsford the cryptic message: 'Zulus attacking. Cannot move at present.'

The Zulu regiments were by now pouring down from the plateau. Shepstone's native horsemen were swept back on the camp by the Right Horn; the Chest drove straight at the camp, while the Left Horn enveloped Colonel Durnford's force, still fighting briskly, in a dongá (dried river bed) to the south-west of Conical Kopje (a small hill). Durnford's men poured a concentrated fire into the Zulu ranks and pinned many down in front of them. The main force in the Left Horn, however, trotted past Durnford and pressed on towards the camp. Eventually Durnford pulled his surviving troops back to a position in the Saddle (a hollow between Isandhlwana Mountain and Stony Hill) where he prepared to make a final stand.

Colonel Pulleine, back at the camp, had now made his final troop arrangements. Because of the speed of the Zulu advance it had not been possible to throw up any proper defensive system; there was not even a laager of waggons end-to-end which the Boers had found so effective during earlier conflicts. The result was that 800 British troops and about 900 African auxiliaries had to man a perimeter of such length that their thin red line was stretched to breaking point. With Isandhlwana mountain at their backs, however, and a boulder-strewn slope before them up which the Zulus would have to attack, the British forces could at least fire into the enemy's ranks from a relatively advantageous position.

For a while the Martini-Henry rifles sent volley after volley crashing into the Zulu host, and although the metal barrels of the firearms started to overheat as usual, substantial casualties were inflicted. Some men of the 24th, indeed, were in a relaxed mood, laughing among themselves as they fired at their opponents. But the British defences were in fact about to cave in. The Natal Kaffirs pitted against the ruthless warriors of the umCijo regiment at a bend in the line (called the Knuckle) between Isandhlwana Mountain and the Saddle, were beginning to run out of ammunition; the 300 auxiliaries had a mere thirty rifles between them and only five rounds of ammunition each; moreover, they entertained a mortal dread of their opponents, descended as they were from the warriors of the mighty Shaka. The British infantrymen, despite their earlier confidence, were little better placed : in the rush to defend the camp many of them had failed to pick up their quota of seventy rounds each; worse still, the regiment's reserve ammunition was mostly stored in heavy wooden boxes fastened by two copper bands held in place by nine large screws. In the fluster and crash of the battle, orderlies, batmen and grooms, unable to find screwdrivers and heedless of the protests of the quartermasters, hacked and prised at the ammunition boxes with axes and bayonets. But their feverish efforts were to no avail, and slowly the crackle of British rifle fire abated as ammunition ran out.

At this point the umCijo regiment followed by the isaNgqu and umHlanga, hurled themselves at the wavering Natal Kaffirs. The war cry 'uSuthu! uSuthu!' echoed from the rocks and blended with the noise of thousands of assegais being rattled against cowhide shields. Stricken with fear the native auxiliaries turned and fled, sweeping aside their cursing officers, and carrying with them other auxiliary troops in the camp itself. As the Natal Kaffirs made for the safety of Rorke's Drift they left a 300-yard breach in the north-east of the defensive line. The Zulu horde poured through this gap, butchering all the British troops in their path, until every knot of redcoated resistance had been wiped out.

While this catastrophe overwhelmed the men of the 24th, Colonel Durnford and seventy men stood in a tight circle at the Saddle and fired their final rounds at the enemy. These men then fought the Zulu warriors with bayonets, clubbed carbines and even assegais, until the last trooper had fallen.

As the British defences collapsed in ruins and the Zulus rampaged through the camp looting, and finishing off pockets of resistance, Colonel Pulleine handed over the regimental colours to Lieutenant Melvill, who was pulling out, and then calmly sat down in a tent and began writing. Nobody will ever know what Pulleine found himself compelled to write, for a Zulu broke into the tent and plunged a stabbing assegai into his chest.

The Battle of Isandhlwana was ended. Fifty-five Europeans and a few hundred native auxiliaries managed to escape to Rorke's Drift from where they bore the terrible news into Natal causing the panic-stricken colonists to hastily barricade their homesteads. Over 600 men of the 24th, and 300 other

Europeans, were slaughtered at Isandhlwana, sacrificed to the stealthy approach and the disciplined assault of the Zulu impis, as well as to Lord Chelmsford's failure to detect the approaching enemy. Colonel Durnford, too, must bear heavy censure for not taking command of the camp, since he was senior to Pulleine, and also for leading a considerable proportion of the best troops *out* of the camp towards the hidden Zulu army.

One of the survivors of the catastrophe was Lieutenant Smith-Dorrien, later to become a distinguished general and to serve at the Battle of Mons in 1914. His account of the battle and especially of his escape, written at Rorke's Drift on 25 January, gives a unique taste of the confusion as the survivors fled for safety:

Before we knew where we were they came right into the camp, assegaing everybody right and left. Everybody then who had a horse turned to fly. The enemy were going at a kind of very fast half-walk and half-run. On looking round we saw that we were completely surrounded and that the road to Rorke's Drift was cut off. The place where they seemed thinnest was where we all made for. Everybody went pell-mell over ground covered with huge boulders and rocks until we got to a deep spruit or gulley. How the horses got over I have no idea. I was riding a broken-kneed old crock which did not belong to me, and which I expected to go on its head every minute. We had to go bang through them at the spruit. Lots of our men were killed there. I had some marvellous escapes, and was firing away at them with my revolver as I galloped along. The ground there down to the river was so broken that the Zulus went as fast as the horses, and kept killing all the way. There were very few white men; they were nearly all mounted niggers of ours flying. This lasted till we came to a kind of precipice down to the River Buffalo. I jumped off and led my horse down. There was a poor fellow of the mounted infantry (a private) struck through the arm, who said as I passed that if I could bind up his arm and stop the bleeding he would be all right. I accordingly took out my handkerchief and tied up his arm. Just as I had done it, Major Smith of the Artillery came down by me wounded, saying 'for God's sake, get on man; the Zulus are on top of us'. I had done all I could for the wounded man and so turned to jump on my horse. Just as I was doing so the horse went with a bound to the bottom of the precipice, being struck with an assegai. I gave up all hope, as the Zulus were all round me, finishing off the wounded, the man I had helped and Major Smith among the number. However, with the strong hope that everybody clings to that some accident would turn up, I rushed off on foot and plunged into the river, which was little better than a roaring torrent. I was being carried down the stream at a tremendous pace, when a loose horse came by me and I got hold of his tail and he landed me safely on the other bank; but I was too tired to stick to him and get on his back. I got up again and rushed on and was several times knocked over by our mounted niggers, who would not get out of my way, then up a tremendous hill, with my wet clothes and boots full of water. About twenty Zulus got over the water and followed us up the hill, but, I am thankful to say, they had not their firearms. Crossing the river, however, the Zulus on the opposite side kept firing at us as we went up the hill and killed several of the niggers round me. I was the only white man to be seen until I came to one who had been kicked by his horse, and could not mount. I put him on his horse and lent him my knife. He said he would catch me a horse. Directly he was up he went clean away. A few Zulus followed us for about three miles across the river, but they had no guns, and I had a revolver, which I kept letting them know. Also the mounted niggers stopped from time to time and kept firing at them. They did not come in close and finally stopped altogether.

Well, to cut it short, I struggled into Helpmakaar, about twenty miles off, at nightfall, to find a few men who had escaped, about ten or twenty, with others who had been entrenched in a wagon laager. We sat up all night expecting attack. The next day, there was a dense fog all day, nearly as bad as night, and we could not make out what had happened to everybody. I was dead beat, of course, but on 24th January I struggled down to Rorke's Drift, which had been gallantly defended for a whole night against the Zulus by a single company, to find that the General [Chelmsford] and remainder of the column had arrived all right. I am there now in a laager. We keep a tremendous look-out, and sit up all night expecting attack. It has been raining for the last three hours and did so all night. The men have no coats or anything, all being taken by the Zulus. We shall have another dreadful night of it tonight, I expect, lying on the wet ground. I have just had to drop this for a minute for one of our numerous alarms. I have no time for more now. What we are to do for transport I have not the faintest idea, the Zulus having captured 107 wagons and about 2,000 oxen, mules, horses, etc. However, we must begin to work again to get fresh transport together. I thank God I am alive and well, having a few bruises.

Lieutenant Smith-Dorrien's references to the heroic defence of Rorke's Drift by Lieutenant Chard's Company is an important one, for the action provided a flash of encouragement in the gloomy aftermath of Isandhlwana. Lieutenants Chard and Broomhead had marshalled some 350 men, of which the indispensable nucleus was 'B' Company of the 24th Regiment, in defence of the mission station at Rorke's Drift and had held off over 4,000 Zulus led by Cetshwayo's half brother Dabulamanzi. This minor epic in Victorian military history prompted a pragmatic and down-to-earth assessment by one of the rank-and-file enlisted men who had fought in the action. Writing to his brother in Cape Town, Robert Head put the momentous events in his own perspective:

I now send you these few lines to inform you of what I daresay you will have seen in the paper before you receive this we under Lieut Chard and Broomhead had a nice

night of it at Rodke's Drift I call it I never shall forget the
same place about as long as I live I daresay the old Fool in
command will make a great fuss over our two officers
commanding our company in keeping the Zulu Buck back
with the private soldier what will he get nothing only he
may get the praise of the public Now I shall if God spares
me live and see dear old England again I shall find what I
say to be true so now as I had to give a shilling for this bit
of paper you will only be able to know I am ready and
willing to lose my life to win back for our sister battalion
1-/24 renown so kindest love to all I am jolly short of a
[pipe] and bacca
    your loving brother Bob Head

While the reputation of British arms was being in part re-
trieved at Rorke's Drift, the northern flanking column under
General Wood was advancing from Kambula, where it had set up
a fortified camp, towards Hlobane. The southern flanking
column, led by Colonel Pearson, had crossed the Lower Drift of
the Tugela and had pushed on to the mission station of Eshowe.

The southern column had enjoyed an easy march until 22
January. It consisted of the 2nd Battalion of the East Kent
Regiment (the 'Buffs'), the single-battalion 99th Regiment, 200
sailors from the Naval Brigade, 2,256 Natal Kaffirs, and 312
mounted men; there were four pieces of artillery, and the new-
fangled, ten-barrelled Gatling gun which boasted a remarkable
rate of fire and was about to go into action for the first time with
the British army.

On 22 January, as the column drew near to Eshowe, they
encountered a Zulu force of over 6,000 men among spurs and
ravines close by a ridge called Majia's Hill. Fortunately Pearson
was able to get his artillery (including the Gatling gun) into
action, and his infantrymen into good positions. A withering
volume of fire poured into the Zulu impis as they advanced towards the British forces. Within an hour and a half it was all
over: ten men of the invading column were killed and sixteen
wounded, but over 350 Zulus had died. The impis withdrew.

Pearson marched on to Eshowe, which he reached on the following morning, and promptly set about fortifying it. His men had so far only cause for self-congratulation. But on 26 January African runners brought the first garbled, but ominous, news of the engagement at Isandhlwana four days before. On 28 January a runner arrived with a telegram from Lord Chelmsford. It did not make happy reading :

> Consider all my instructions as cancelled, and act in whatever manner you think most desirable in the interests of the column under your command. Should you consider the garrison of Eshowe as too far advanced to be fed with safety, you can withdraw it. Hold, however, if possible, the post on the Zulu side of the Lower Tugela. You must be prepared to have the whole Zulu force down upon you. Do away with tents, and let the men take shelter under the wagons which will then be in position for defence and hold so many more supplies.

Clearly a major disaster had occurred somewhere to the northwest, and evidently Chelmsford had also belatedly absorbed the Boer conviction that security lay with the formation of a laager. Apart from that Pearson was on his own. Eventually a council of war voted for sending all the mounted men and the 2nd Regiment of the Natal Kaffirs back to Fort Tenedos – the post on the Zulu side of the Lower Tugela that Chelmsford had wanted maintained. Pearson remained at Eshowe with a garrison reduced to 1,300 European troops and about 400 African drivers and auxiliaries. Messages dribbled through from Chelmsford, each one more discouraging than the last. The Zulus moved freely about the surrounding countryside, and eventually closed in round the garrison. On 11 February the last frightened African runner reached Eshowe; Chelmsford made it clear that Pearson could expect no reinforcements for six weeks at least. There were no more messages after that : Eshowe was under siege.

The central column had been defeated and partly wiped out. Now the southern flanking column was shut up at Eshowe. Only

Evelyn Wood's northern force was able to move freely. On 20 March Lord Chelmsford proposed that Wood should cause a diversion in the Hlobane area and thus draw off some of the impis surrounding Eshowe. Wood accordingly sent two columns against Zulu forces on the main plateau of the Hlobane system. The first column was led by Major Redvers Buller (who was later, as Commander-in-Chief in South Africa, to blunder his way through the first disastrous months of the Boer War of 1899–1902); it consisted of 400 irregular horsemen, including thirty of Piet Uys's commando and seventy men from Captain Raaf's Transvaal Rangers; there were also nearly 300 African auxiliaries (known as Wood's Irregulars). The European horsemen were a formidable bunch : Uys led Afrikaners of proven toughness and resiliance; Piet Raaf, who was remarkably and decidedly pro-British, commanded a troop of whom it was said uncharitably but not inaccurately that 'a more forbidding lot of mixed Hottentots and the scum of the diamond fields was never collected together outside a prison wall'.

The second column was led by Wood himself and comprised about 300 African auxiliaries and 200 tribesmen of a well-disposed local chieftain named Uhamu. The first column was ordered to scale the Hlobane plateau at the far, eastern, end; the second column would approach via the western ascent, and together the two forces would rout the Zulus stationed on the plateau. At first the twin assault went reasonably well. Buller's men plodded onto Hlobane through a foul storm. The western column also struggled onto the plateau, prodded on by Wood from the rear. Sporadic fighting accompanied these manoeuvres.

But before Wood could consolidate the position he saw a huge body of Zulus bearing down on Hlobane from the south-east. The impis were on their way to attack the camp at Kambula, but had now swung towards their newly revealed foes. Among the 20,000 warriors was Cetshwayo's brother Dabulamanzi, and Mnyamana the King's leading induna; the umCijo and umHlanga regiments that had triumphed earlier at Isandhlwana were among the host.

As Buller's and Wood's men tried to descend from Hlobane in order to retreat to Kambula, the Zulus attacked them from the rocks that fringed the narrow downward paths. Troopers and horses were stabbed and hacked, and many of the native auxiliaries that reached the plain were cut down by the Left Horn of the Zulu attack. Nearly a hundred European horsemen were killed, as well as scores of Natal Kaffirs. Among those who died was Piet Uys. His brother J.J. Uys described what happened:

> On Friday March 28, 1879, the caves of Hlobane where-in [the] impi were entrenched were stormed and carried by my brother and other military officers and men. The mountain was then surrounded by about 35,000 [sic] Zulus who had lain concealed during the storming of the Hlobane stronghold. Our people, seeing that the Zulus had surrounded the mountain, ran to the south-west to ride off there, and gave no heed to my brother's orders and those of other officers. The mountain had no proper way down and the path, such as it was, was well-nigh im-passable for horses. My brother, who is known to us all to be a man without fear, remained behind to help and assist those behind to escape. He contributed to that end and many Zulus in the attacking party at Hlobane fell to his unerring aim with the rifle. He saw his eldest son on the dreadful mountain having difficulty with two led horses and went to his aid. The horses broke away and father and son got separated from each other. When the son came to a level place he looked back and saw a Zulu plunge an assegai into his father's body.

After their triumph at Hlobane the Zulus advanced towards Kambula. Here a bloody battle developed and Mnyamana's regiments were hurled back leaving 2,000 dead behind them. The defenders of Kambula lost a mere thirty men. Although the suc-cessful repulse of the Zulus at Kambula could be set against the scrambled retreat from Hlobane, British arms had suffered yet another strategic setback. None of the three columns sent against Cetshwayo's kingdom in January had penetrated anywhere near

Ulundi, and all had, in fact, been either defeated or contained by their opponents. The British fell back dispirited. The first invasion of Zululand was over.

But the Zulus had paid dearly for their victories. Over 6,000 of them had already perished, and all the regiments had now been blooded with a vengeance. They had also learned that, properly organized and supplied, sufficient numbers of British infantry could decimate their ranks. Even the lion-like courage of the heirs of Shaka could not prevail against the massed Martini-Henry rifles. Cetshwayo knew what price his impis had paid, and tried pathetically to negotiate with the British before they attacked him again.

It was of no avail. By June, Lord Chelmsford, with a reinforced and reorganized army, was on the move once more, despite the flood of hostile criticism that his earlier failure had provoked in the British parliament and press, and throughout the European communities in southern Africa. But his days as commander were numbered. The British Prime Minister Disraeli planned to replace both the 'cowed and confused' Chelmsford and Governor Sir Bartle Frere with one abundantly talented, many-sided figure – Sir Garnet Wolseley, conqueror of the Ashanti, brilliant master of the small-scale campaign.

Before Wolseley could supersede Chelmsford, however, the latter had avenged his humiliation at Isandhlwana by breaking the impis at the Battle of Ulundi in July 1879. The royal Kraal was burned to ashes, and Cetshwayo's power was devoured in the flames. Wolseley took over from Chelmsford and proceeded to hunt Cetshwayo down. The captured King was sent to captivity in Cape Town wearing a European suit and a broad-brimmed hat. To their everlasting credit the British authorities resisted a business offer from the American impresario P.T. Barnum to include the fallen ruler in his show.

But Cetshwayo's suit, hat and gloves had their own symbolism. The Zulu nation had been overthrown, and the House of Shaka destroyed; Zululand was broken into thirteen separate kingdoms; more than 8,000 warriors had died. The colonists of Natal and the Transvaal, both British and Boer, could now live and flourish without the brooding menace of the impis across their borders. But the price had been high : 1,430 Europeans (including the Prince Imperial, son of the ex-Emperor Napoleon III) and nearly one thousand Natal Kaffirs had been killed; 1,385 British soldiers had been invalided home; moreover the war had cost the British £5,230,323. In view of the fact that one side had fought with assegais and knobkerries and the other with breech-loading rifles and modern field pieces these losses reflected little credit upon the victors.

Part V
The First Boer War 1880–1

I do not feel anxious, for I know these people [the Transvaalers] cannot be united.

> The Governor of the Transvaal,
> Sir Owen Lanyon, to
> General Sir George Colley,
> December 1880.

> You English fight to die; we Boers fight to live.
> Afrikaner saying.

> What can you expect from fighting on a Sunday?
> Commandant-General Piet Joubert
> after the Battle of Majuba Hill.

12
Rebellion, 1880

Boer indignation at the British annexation of the Transvaal was not assuaged by the eventual destruction of Zulu power. Many Afrikaners, indeed, had hoped that if Lord Chelmsford's army suffered a serious setback in Zululand then the British hold over the Transvaal would be weakened; but this had not happened. The deportment of the Governor of the Transvaal, Colonel Sir William Owen Lanyon, rubbed further salt into the wound. Lanyon was off-hand, arrogant and inclined to despotic practices; he also despised the Boers as a 'semi-civilized people who think of leniency and forbearance as a sign of weakness and fear'. The fact that he proved adept at squeezing taxes out of the notoriously tight-fisted Afrikaners was another reason for his, and the regime's, unpopularity in the Transvaal.

Nor did the advent of the triumphant Wolseley, after his mopping-up in Zululand, quieten Afrikaner resentment. Wolseley, the newly-appointed High Commissioner of South-East Africa, swaggered into Pretoria in October 1879 and announced that the Vaal river would flow back into the Drakensburg before the Transvaal regained its independence. In fact Wolseley was genuinely confident that the Transvaal would remain a permanent part of the Empire. He predicted, with eerie accuracy, that great mineral deposits would be found, and that British settlers would pour into the province in such numbers that they would outnumber the Afrikaners. He advised the Colonial Secretary in London, Hicks Beach, that it would be expedient to maintain a small garrison in the Transvaal for peace-keeping duties. Not that he showed much concern at Boer complaints, telling Hicks Beach that 'They are given to more boasting and tall talk than Americans, but at heart they are cowards.'

Rarely had so staggering a misconception been enunciated with greater confidence; rarely has the judgement of so highly-placed and successful an officer been proved so disastrously wrong so rapidly. Within a few weeks of Wolseley's arrival at Pretoria he got a taste of Boer discontent when a meeting of 6,000 Transvaalers at Wonderfontein passed resolutions demanding independence and affirming their determination to fight for such an end. Wolseley arrested two of the leaders of this gathering, Marthinus Pretorius and William Bok, but was later induced to release them. The Transvaalers had also greeted with derision a new constitution which packed the Executive and Legislative Councils with British officials and nominees.

The sham constitution was further proof to the Afrikaners that they could expect no real share in the government of their fallen republic. Equally irksome was the presence of the British garrisons. The redcoated enlisted men had acquired a reputation for drunkenness, abuse of property, and clumsy attempts to pollute the virtue of Afrikaner womenfolk. Fuel was added to this smouldering, though parochial, fire when William Russell, the world famous war correspondent whose letters from the Crimea and the Indian Mutiny had produced such an effect at home, denounced the conduct of British troops in the Transvaal in a letter published in the *Daily Telegraph* in November 1879.

Wolseley fumed against Russell's attacks, asking indignantly

'What could have made him so treacherously vicious?' Still, it was undeniable that the British garrisons provided daily reminders of the Transvaal's subordination to Whitehall. Wolseley, for his own part, was anxious to reduce the number of troops – though chiefly to convince his superiors in London that the Transvaal was truly pacified, and that he could move on to new glories. He accordingly resented Sir Bartle Frere's continuing preoccupation with achieving federation throughout southern Africa since this implied the maintenance of substantial Imperial forces in the Transvaal. Wolseley accused Frere of 'Napoleonic delirium', and suspected him of wanting to regain his lost position as High Commissioner for the whole of South Africa, since Wolseley's appointment had stripped Sir Bartle of responsibility for South-East Africa. Wolseley therefore opposed 'Sir Bottle Beer's' grandiose military plans on the one hand, and on the other began to reduce the Transvaal garrison.

In April 1880 events in Britain strengthened Wolseley's hand. The Liberals were swept to a crushing victory in the general election; Disraeli fell, and Gladstone returned to 10 Downing Street. During the election campaign Gladstone had heaped telling and self-righteous abuse on Disraeli for his imperial adventures in Afghanistan, Zululand and the Transvaal. This Gladstonian invective had achieved wide currency in the Transvaal, and the Afrikaners came to believe that a Liberal victory at the polls would mean a speedy return to self-government. So convinced were they, that the long awaited general assembly of discontented burghers scheduled for 6 April 1880 was postponed.

Wolseley also had every reason to welcome a Liberal administration with a well known dislike of excessive military expenditure; it enabled him to hasten the troop withdrawals from the Transvaal. At the end of the Zulu War there were more than 10,000 British regular troops stationed in South-East Africa. Now regiment after regiment sailed for home. By the time Wolseley left the Transvaal in April 1880 there were only three infantry battalions and a cavalry regiment left in the colony. His successor as

High Commissioner for South-East Africa, his friend and protégé Sir George Pomeroy Colley, ordered further reductions. By the end of the year there were about 1,800 regular troops in the Transvaal: 500 of them were in the garrison at Pretoria, and the rest scattered in five outlying posts; there was not a single squadron of Imperial cavalry in a country where the Afrikaner males were renowned for their fine horsemanship as well as for their skill with firearms.

While the shaky British administration in the Transvaal was being systematically stripped of its military support, the Gladstone government proceeded to deny it the tattered remnants of its former credibility. In June 1880 the Prime Minister, replying to the representatives of an Afrikaner committee headed by the subtle and intransigent Paul Kruger, ex-Vice-President of the fallen republic, said: 'Our judgement is that the Queen cannot be advised to relinquish her sovereignty over the Transvaal.' Gladstone's *volte face* owed much to pressure from his ill-assorted Cabinet colleagues: the Whigs, like Lord Kimberley the Colonial Secretary, argued that the best (and cheapest) way of keeping a grip on affairs in southern Africa was to press ahead with the federation programme; some Radicals, like Sir Charles Dilke, claimed that a continuing British presence in the Transvaal would serve to protect the Bantu from Afrikaner brutality.

To the Transvaalers, however, the delicate political calculations behind Gladstone's shift of position were immaterial. Like the British Radical MP Leonard Courtney they could see no difference between Gladstone's South African policy and that of Disraeli. Joseph Chamberlain, another Radical MP and a Junior Minister (who was later, ironically, to push through the South African War of 1899–1902) claimed that the Transvaalers would 'worry this country into granting independence'.

He was right. Urged on by militants like Kruger and Piet Joubert, the Afrikaners began to prepare for an armed uprising against the British authorities. Events seemed to be going their way: the remaining British garrisons were prey to indiscipline and desertion (nearly 400 soldiers deserted during 1880); morale was generally low and the consumption of cheap alcohol high; some Transvaalers, indeed, even believed that certain British detachments would support them in their fight for independence. Another encouraging development for the Afrikaners lay in the Basuto rebellion of September 1880 which prompted Governor Lanyon to dispatch 300 experienced volunteers to cope with the disturbances; these volunteers would have provided invaluable mounted support for the British forces in the Transvaal. Meanwhile the Afrikaners began stealthily to organize themselves into commando units for the impending struggle.

The rebellion broke out over taxes. The Afrikaners were at the best of times difficult to tax; Governor Lanyon gave much thought to improving the means of tax collection. In November the Transvaalers rigged up a test case in which Piet Bezuidenhout of Potchefstroom was charged by the authorities with owing £27 5s in tax arrears. Brought before the magistrates, Bezuidenhout agreed to pay £14, but asked provocatively that the sum should be held over until the republican government was restored. He was then ordered to pay the costs of the case which were assessed at £13 5s, thus presenting him with the original debt of £27 5s. Bezuidenhout refused to pay up and his waggon was impounded. On 11 November the waggon was put up for public auction at Potchefstroom. A rebellious crowd assembled and when the sheriff climbed aboard the waggon to begin the auction, Piet Cronje, a fiery future leader of Afrikaner nationalism, kicked him aside saying 'Away with you, you Government officials, we don't recognize you!'

This incident was, in itself, no more than an undignified scuffle in the South African equivalent to the Wild West, with Potchefstroom as the venue rather than Dodge City. But to Kruger and the Transvaal militants Piet Bezuidenhout and his waggon were powerful symbols of defiance; it was appropriate that, instead of a gauntlet, the Afrikaners should have cast down – the trek waggon! Plans were now laid for holding a great rally at Paardekraal on 8 December.

It was of no avail that Lanyon declared the meeting illegal,

4,000 Afrikaners descended on Paadekraal and there demanded the restoration of the republic (though they were prepared to let Britain control its foreign policy). Until this happy consummation could be effected they elected a triumvirate to rule them; the chosen three were Kruger, Joubert and Pretorius. Then, after each man had placed a stone on a great cairn to signify the assembly's unity of purpose, the Transvaalers dispersed. But, ominously for the British, they broke up into commando groups according to a prearranged strategy.

On 15 December the first shots were fired at Potchefstroom between jeering Transvaalers and men of the Royal Scots Fusiliers. In Pretoria, Governor Lanyon still dismissed the rebels as 'inflated toads', though he also offered to grant 'any reasonable requests in the direction of representative institutions'. In London, the Colonial Secretary, Lord Kimberley, dispatched reinforcements, while putting out feelers for an honourable retreat from the confrontation. Just across the border in Natal, General Colley confidently marshalled his small army, while his opponents swung into rapid action, seizing Heidelburg as their capital, and surrounding the scattered British garrisons. War in the Transvaal, for so long dismissed as impossible by the blindly optimistic Lanyon, was about to begin in earnest.

13
Three in a Row: the First Defeats

The confrontation between the rebellious Transvaalers and the British Empire seemed, at first sight, ludicrous. A force of less than 8,000, farmers for the most part, was chancing its arm against regular Imperial battalions; behind the redcoats were the thousands of troops that could be poured in as reinforcements, as well as all the paraphernalia of modern war – up-to-date artillery, good equipment, staff officers, a commissariat.

Yet appearances belied the reality. The Afrikaners were arguably the most skilful, determined and intelligent mounted infantry in the world. Their horsemanship was easy and confident, as if, like the centaurs of ancient mythology, they were half-horse half-man. They were able to fire their rifles from the saddle with great accuracy. The extraordinary marksmanship of the Afrikaner owed a great deal to regular practice and a superb judgement of distance. Moreover, ammunition was scarce and treasured accordingly; every bullet had to count. The Boers lavished care on their horses and upon their rifles, which were nearly always modern – Winchester repeaters, Enfield Sniders, Westley-Richardses and so on.

Though their rifles were well-oiled and their horses in fine fettle, the Afrikaners themselves looked more like a rabble of tramps than an efficient fighting force. Their tall frames were clothed in the rough corduroy, flannel and animal skins that they wore for farm work; their hair and beards were often long and tangled. They carried, apart from their precious rifles, a bandolier stuffed with cartridges, and saddle bags for essential supplies. One staple diet was biltong (strips of dried meat); biltong hardly ever went bad, and it was claimed that a five-pound piece could sustain a man for ten days.

British observers derided the unkempt high veld Boers, but there was, in fact, little enough to laugh at. Their dark, patched clothes provided excellent camouflage; their lack of military professionalism was a first-rate advantage in campaigns which required ingenuity and stealth; though they elected their commandants, and could join or leave the commando as they thought fit, they felt a loyalty to their units that was every bit as fierce as regimental pride but based upon democratic choice rather than upon the dull obedience of enlisted men paid a shilling a day. Above all, the Afrikaners made unbeatable use of the terrain; preferring to fire from cover, scorning story-book heroics, no Boer wished to die in the last ditch when he could slip away and fight another day. He was kept supplied by the womenfolk, and by the young, the aged and the sick.

In December 1880 the Afrikaners mobilized nearly 8,000 men within forty-eight hours. Only those under sixteen years old and over sixty were exempt, together with pastors, officials, schoolteachers and the badly disabled. The Transvaal was divided into twelve electoral districts: each district provided a commando; within the district two or three elected Veld Kornets (field cornets) supervised mobilization and organized supply, assisted in the latter activity by the women and youngsters. Thus the whole nation was closely involved in the war from first to last. Morale was high, and many believed that 'General Jesus' was actively engaged on their side. More practically, they were led into the field by Commandant-General 'Slim' (crafty) Piet Joubert, a resourceful and shrewd campaigner, whose second-in-command, Nicholas Smit was soon to be described (by an admiring General Butler) as 'one of the ablest leaders of mounted infantry that have appeared in modern war'.

Rather than the raggle-taggle Afrikaners it was the brightly-uniformed British troops that best deserved ridicule and contempt. The Imperial battalions tramped across the veld, making little attempt to disguise their noisy progress, each infantryman carrying far more equipment than was normally strapped onto a Boer's horse. The heavy-recoiling Martini-Henry rifle was not intrinsically inferior to the Afrikaner's weapons, but was generally in less capable hands. Bayonets were considered a joke by the Boers – for why should they allow themselves to get close enough to be skewered by one? Above all, the rules and regulations of British campaigning seemed absurd to their opponents, most of whom had never opened a military text-book in their lives and who preferred improvised action to fixed reactions.

The British got an early taste of what was in store for them on 20 December 1880. Colonel Anstruther, with 235 men of the 94th Foot, some medical corps men and a few service wives and children, was marching 190 miles from Lydenberg, in the eastern Transvaal, to relieve Pretoria which was invested by the Afrikaners. Anstruther's progress was slow and at the same time over-confident – since he neglected to reconnoitre ahead properly.

Shortly after midday on 20 December the straggling column approached a small watercourse called Bronkhurst Spruit. The band was blaring out 'Kiss me mother, kiss your darling daughter', and the travel-stained troops were eating local peaches. Suddenly Anstruther spotted horsemen upon a ridge some 300 yards ahead; others were behind cover on each side of the road. The men numbered about 200 and belonged to Franz Joubert's commando. An Afrikaner rode up to the Colonel and handed him a message signed by the newly-designated triumvirate (Kruger, Piet Joubert and Pretorius). This note demanded that Anstruther halt where he was, until Governor Lanyon replied to a letter from the triumvirate informing him of the reconstitution of the Transvaal Republic. More threateningly the note added that if Anstruther persisted in his march it would be considered an act of war.

What was any self-respecting officer of the Queen to do in such circumstances, but march on to Pretoria? Anstruther huffed and puffed, and told the emissary to 'do as you like!' Then he waited for a reply, as the horseman rode back. But within minutes the Afrikaners had closed round the British column. Anstruther ordered his men to move out into skirmishing order, but almost before they could unsling their rifles a murderously accurate fire caught them. Officers and men went down like nine-pins, including the Colonel. The British lost 120 men in killed and wounded; the Afrikaners two killed and five wounded.

Bronkhurst Spruit was a massacre, spiced with treachery, but compounded mainly of over-confidence. Anstruther was formally correct in awaiting a reply to his message, but tactically naive in not ordering his men into battle order. Before dying of his wounds, the Colonel taxed his victorious opponents with an unfair act of war, but the skirmish was already passing into history.

The news of Bronkhurst Spruit struck Governor Lanyon like a bolt from the blue, and he wrote querulously to General Colley that 'I must confess the situation is a most puzzling one, both to me and to everyone who should know the Boer character'. Colley, however, put things into clearer perspective in a letter to his sister, saying

> The disaster has not only been a painful loss to us of many good officers and men, but has changed the whole aspect of affairs – a sort of Isandhlwana on a smaller scale. Had the 94th beaten off their assailants, as I still think they should have done if proper precautions had been taken on the march, the garrison of Pretoria would have been so far reinforced, and the Boers discouraged, that I doubt if Colonel Bellairs [the commander at Pretoria] would

have allowed himself to be invested at all, but think he would probably have taken the field at once and very likely dispersed the Boers.

Colley's cool appraisal of the disaster could not, however, dispel its effects. British authority throughout the Transvaal simply disintegrated after Bronkhurst Spruit. The 1500 garrison troops were quickly hemmed in by the determined and triumphant Afrikaners and were to play no significant part in the subsequent war. In Europe and in the United States there was much satisfaction at British discomfiture, and the Transvaal was generally seen as struggling gallantly for its rightful independence. The British press, with a few exceptions, stormed against the rebels : *The Times* called Bronkhurst Spruit 'a cold-blooded murder of British troops . . . a deed worthy of savages'; other newspapers declared that the insurrection must be put down at whatever cost. This was all very well, but who was to crush the insurgents and replace the *vierkleur* (the Republic's flag) with the Union Jack? There was of course only one man in a position to do it – Major-General Sir George Pomeroy Colley, High Commissioner for South-East Africa, Governor of Natal, and Commander-in-Chief of the British forces in the Transvaal and Natal.

Colley was a bookish soldier, very much cast in the same mould as his mentor Garnet Wolseley. He had passed brilliantly through Sandhurst and the Staff College, and had served in the China War of 1860, in the Ashanti War (under Wolseley), and in India in 1876. His advancement had been irresistible, and had owed as much to his own undeniable capabilities as to Wolseley's consistent backing. Colley preferred painting to fox-hunting, and the leisurely perusal of Ruskin to gambling. But his sensitivity and forbearance, though admirable qualities, were less useful on the battlefield than an unwavering urge to conquer. Moreover, before he succeeded to Wolseley's high offices in 1880, he had always had a gifted and masterful superior to lean on. Now he was on his own, and in the end this was to prove insufficient.

On Christmas Day 1880 Colley received the harrowing news of the disaster at Bronkhurst Spruit. It was now up to him to move in relief of the six beleaguered garrisons in the Transvaal. But even after scouring Natal for troops he was only able to muster a mere thousand – and these included no Imperial cavalry. If he succeeded in relieving the British garrison he would then release nearly 3,000 Imperial troops and loyal volunteers – there were nearly 2,000 at Pretoria to start off with. On the other hand, he could stay put and await the arrival of reinforcements that had already been summoned from India. Yet if he did this he would greatly increase the risk of the garrisons falling, and the Transvaalers would have won a great propaganda victory to set beside their military triumphs.

Colley decided to advance into the Transvaal, though he spent nearly a month assembling his puny invasion force at Newcastle in Natal. Eventually he boasted twelve companies of infantry drawn from the 58th and 2/21 Regiments of Foot, and from 3/60th Rifles; they were all short-service men, lacking in confidence and experience, and mostly very poor shots. There were also 120 sailors borrowed from British warships anchored in Durban harbour. The artillery consisted of two seven-pounders, four nine-pounders and some rocket tubes. Though Colley technically commanded 150 horsemen, they were mostly volunteers from the local police force or from the infantry, and in neither case could they be described as cavalrymen.

At last, on 24 January 1881, Colley was able to march out of Newcastle. Rejecting less obvious routes he made straight for Laing's Nek, the pass in the Drakensberg on the main road from Natal to the Transvaal. On 26 January the British force trudged through rain and mist to a farm named Mount Prospect, four miles south of Laing's Nek. On the next morning the troops squinted under a weak sun at the great grassy ridge that confronted them. The high rampart ran for six miles, dividing northern Natal from the southern Transvaal, but at its centre it dipped and here was the saddle, raised some 500 feet above the plain, and called Laing's Nek. On either side of the Nek there were daunting heights which, if manned, would command the pass. To the left of Laing's Nek the ground rose steeply in huge steps until it was crowned by a flat-topped mountain called Majuba, the hill of the doves.

Colley also saw through his binoculars that the Transvaalers were already strung out along the ridge, and busily digging in. Feeling, strangely, that destiny had placed him there at that particular time, he made his plans for the assault. He decided to attack and turn the Boers' extreme left flank and thence dispose of their entrenchments. The plan was probably as good as any other, but it was based on an over-hasty assessment of the terrain.

Early the next morning, 28 January, the assault column moved off under brilliant sunshine. From their high vantage point the Transvaalers saw the sun winking on the bayonets of the ten spruce companies of infantry; they also saw the 150 irregular horsemen in blue uniform, the rocket tubes, the four field guns trundling behind.

The troops made for the left flank of the entrenchments. At the foot of the vital ridge Colley suddenly realized that its upper slopes were dominated by a spur jutting out from the right. If this spur could be cleared by cavalry, then the infantrymen could advance without serious opposition. Colley paused to issue new orders. By 10 am all was ready, and the artillery began its bombardment of the Afrikaner positions. Five companies of the 58th began to clamber up the ridge, but their progress was slow, and the mounted troops were impatiently ordered to attack by their commander Major Brownlow. The first squadron of cavalry managed to scramble to the edge of the Afrikaner trenches before they were shot to pieces; the second squadron panicked at the slaughter, turned tail and scampered down the slope with Major Brownlow's curses ringing in their ears.

The failure of the hotch potch cavalry force probably lost the battle, for the Boers had in fact been shaken by the first squadron's approach and a second determined assault might well have turned their left flank. But having repulsed these irresolute horsemen, the Afrikaners now had the glorious opportunity to pick off the men of the 58th as they struggled towards them some 400 yards away. What happened next was compounded equally of tragedy and farce.

The 480 officers and men of the 58th approached the crest of the ridge in parade-ground order. In front rode the officers and some of Colley's staff, their naked swords in their hands; behind them toiled the redcoated infantry, shoulder to shoulder, and soaked in sweat; the regimental colours fluttered bravely to the fore, though this was to be the last time that any unit of the British army was to carry colours into battle. Fire from the flanks was bringing a few men stumbling down.

Close to the summit of the ridge the commander of the 58th, Colonel Deane, prepared to lead his men in a final, text-book, assault. He ordered them to fix bayonets, and then yelled at them to charge. Obediently his men lunged towards the rows of rifle barrels that faced them. It was all over in a trice : the 58th were cut down by an appallingly accurate fusilade from the Afrikaner trenches; the officers fell like nine-pins, including General Colley's ADC who died with 'floreat Etona' on his lips. The survivors retired in a remarkably orderly fashion, but they left 150 comrades stretched out on the grassy slopes of the ridge.

The Boers had held Laing's Nek with ridiculous ease, and the discomfited British marched back to their camp at Mount Prospect. The Afrikaners lost a mere fourteen dead and twenty-seven wounded. Their success greatly boosted their confidence in their fight for independence, and emphasized the superiority of their tactics and marksmanship. Colley, licking his wounds, absorbed too well the lessons of the engagement; he now became convinced that bayonet charges were of limited effectiveness, and that forces that held the summit of a hill could decisively repulse any attack. These conclusions were to cost him his life, and the British the whole campaign.

The Liberal government had meanwhile continued to negotiate directly with the rebellious Transvaalers. The Colonial Secretary, Lord Kimberley, had asked President Brand of the

Orange Free State to mediate between the two sides and to inform Kruger that her Majesty's Government did 'not despair of making a satisfactory arrangement' provided that the Transvaalers ceased 'their armed opposition to the Queen's authority'. Naturally enough the rebels saw no need to lay down arms that were being used so triumphantly against the British forces.

For his part, Colley was burning to avenge his defeat at Laing's Nek. There seemed every reason to suppose that his revenge would not be delayed for long, especially since reinforcements were only a few weeks away, and Sir Evelyn Wood was sailing from England to act as Colley's second-in-command. Wood was, like Colley, a member of the influential clique nicknamed the 'Wolseley ring'; he had served in the Ashanti War (1873–4), and had survived the early set-backs of the Zulu War to be in at the kill at the Battle of Ulundi. Colley wrote optimistically to Wood on 4 February 1881 telling him that by 20 February he hoped to have been reinforced by the 15th Hussars, the 2nd Battalion 60th Regiment and the experienced 92nd Regiment. He would then command 2,200 infantry, 450 cavalry and 8 guns and Gatlings.

These schemes were, however, abruptly shattered on 7 February when, as a result of a successful Boer ambush of the mail escort from Newcastle to Mount Prospect, Colley decided to teach the insurgents a sharp lesson. On 8 February he set off with five companies of the 60th Rifles, thirty-eight mounted men, and four field pieces (more than 300 men in all) to march ten miles south down the road towards Newcastle and to accompany a convoy of supplies back to Mount Prospect.

After covering five miles the troops reached a double drift just above the junction of the Ingogo and Harte rivers. Leaving a company of the 60th Rifles with two guns to guard the fords, Colley led his men across the rivers and up a slope towards a small plateau, two miles away, called Schuin's Hooghte. As the vanguard of the column drew near the plateau they saw about a hundred enemy horsemen just over half a mile away to the right. Desperately anxious to scatter the Afrikaners the column waited while two nine-pounders were trained on the stationary horse-men. But the opening salvo, instead of tearing into the Afrikaners, whistled high over their heads; the battery commander had got his ranges wrong!

Far from turning away in terror, the enemy horsemen rode straight towards the British columns; they then took cover in a ravine and directed a heavy fire at their opponents; at the same time they began to outflank the British left. Colley saw that he might soon be cut off, and promptly sent two riders back to the camp at Mount Prospect to call up three companies of the 58th to reinforce the Rifles' company left at the double drift.

The British were soon pinned down by the Afrikaners' accurate fire, which killed or wounded nearly all the horses and eventually silenced the artillery by decimating the gunners and any who came to their assistance. Again the Boers made excellent use of cover, while the British were in more exposed positions and easily picked out by virtue of the white sun helmets and red jackets. As the afternoon wore on the men's throats were parched for want of water. The enemy's rate of fire was so relentless that Colley imagined that his force must be outnumbered by three to one. In fact the Boers at no time possessed more than 300 men, thus making the two sides more or less equal in numbers.

Only towards sundown did the British, to their great relief, see that the Afrikaners were preparing to move off. Heavy rain began to drench the thirsty men, and by seven o'clock the enemy had gone. Two hours later the survivors squelched off under cover of darkness towards the Ingogo and Harte drifts, leaving a large number of wounded to die during the cold and wet night hours. Although eight men were swept away while fording the swollen Ingogo river, Colley's depleted column managed at last to stagger back to Mount Prospect.

Dawn brought a cheerless assessment of the British losses, for 150 of the 300 men who had set out from camp less than twenty-four hours earlier had been lost. Boer casualties numbered eighteen. The guns, however, had been saved (though Colley was sadly disenchanted with their performance at the Battle of

Ingogo), and the inexperienced foot soldiers had resisted stead-fastly during the searing heat of the afternoon's fighting. It was evident, though, that it was the Transvaalers' over-confidence that had allowed the British to escape; Smit, the enemy com-mander, had calculated that Colley's beleaguered force would be incapable of an orderly withdrawal during the terrible night storm, and that the Afrikaners could return to finish them off the next morning. It was this one rare example of enemy carelessness that had saved the British from annihilation. For General Colley, and for the men under his command, the portents remained as ominous as ever.

14
Majuba Hill

The catastrophe of Majuba Hill owed a great deal to the divisions within Gladstone's Cabinet. The three military setbacks of Bronkhurst Spruit, Laing's Nek and the Ingogo merely confirmed the ministerial factions in their convictions : the Radical 'doves' became more determined than ever to press for withdrawal; the Whig 'hawks' believed that the government should not make any concessions until the military situation had been at least partly stabilized.

President Brand of the Orange Free State was meanwhile acting as an intermediary between London and the rebel provisional capital at Heidelburg. Despite his activity, however, it was not until 12 February that General Colley received his first letter from Paul Kruger; the contents of this letter were then passed on to Whitehall. In essence, Kruger offered to negotiate with the British only if the annexation was abandoned and the Imperial troops ordered to withdraw. Gladstone now decided at a Cabinet meeting of 15 February to back the 'doves', and as a result Colley was instructed to inform the Transvaalers that if they stopped 'armed opposition' the government would send a commission to negotiate a settlement and, moreover, that if the rebels approved this proposal the British forces would agree to suspend hostilities.

Colley, not unnaturally, wanted further clarification. In particular he asked Lord Kimberley, the Colonial Secretary, on 16 February whether he was now to leave the Afrikaners in possession of Laing's Nek, which was part of Natal, and to abandon plans to relieve the besieged garrisons. Kimberley telegraphed back that: 'It will be essential that garrisons should be free to provision themselves and peaceful intercourse with them allowed, but we do not mean that you should march to the relief of the garrisons or occupy Laing's Nek if arrangements proceed.'

On 21 February, therefore, Colley sent the Cabinet's proposal that had been formulated on the 15th of the month to Laing's Nek where he believed Kruger to be. He added that if the Afrikaners accepted the proposal within forty-eight hours then he would agree to suspend hostilities. The hours ticked away; the days passed; then, on 24 February, General Smit at Laing's Nek acknowledged receipt of the letter, but pointed out that Kruger had gone to Heidelburg. On 26 February, Colley learnt that Kruger had moved on to Rustenberg and that his reply would be even further delayed.

Colley now found himself in a perplexing quandary. Was Kruger playing for time in the hope that the British situation would continue to deteriorate and the government become more and more anxious to make a settlement? On the other hand, if he waited for Kruger indefinitely the republican triumvirate's authority would grow with the passing of each day, and any remaining Afrikaner waverers would be tempted to throw in their lot with the rebels. Furthermore, the Boer defenders of Laing's Nek were working like moles to throw up more earthworks and strengthen existing ones.

There is also no doubt that Colley was burning to avenge his unhappy failures at Laing's Nek and the Ingogo, and thus to provide some firm evidence that he was indeed one of the Victorian army's up-and-coming commanders. On 26 February, forty-eight hours after General Smit had acknowledged receipt of his letter, Colley decided to take action. It was a decision that was to end in his own death and the ignominious rout of his troops. Nonetheless, given the local military circumstances, Colley was probably right to act as he did.

Also, he had a new and daring plan! He had observed that the table-topped mountain of Majuba, which loomed over the enemy entrenchments at Laing's Nek, had not been permanently occupied by the Boers; for although an enemy picket was sent to the summit during the day, it was withdrawn at night. Colley therefore concluded that if his troops could occupy the summit under cover of darkness they would have gained a decisive advantage. The Afrikaners would either have to abandon their now untenable positions on the Nek, or to fight against opponents enjoying a tactical superiority due to their domination of the summit.

Careful plans were laid for the assault. The Boers were lulled into a false sense of security by the withdrawal of a battalion of the 60th Rifles; there was also a feint to the east of Laing's Nek thus encouraging enemy speculation that the next attack might come from that direction. Colley detailed seven infantry companies and a naval unit (554 men in all) for the march; but, since three companies were to provide a communications and supply link, only some 350 would finally reach the summit. Each man had to carry enough rations to last, at a pinch, for six days, plus 70 rounds of ammunition, a groundsheet, and a greatcoat. Every company had six picks and four shovels. It is clear therefore that Colley anticipated that once his men had dug in they would be supplied and reinforced with comparative ease and that, in all probability, the action would be over soon.

The first stage of the march was a brilliant success. The column set off at 10 pm on the night of 26 February, the troops stumbling beneath their heavy packs and sometimes crawling on all fours as the slope grew steeper. By 3.40 am on Sunday 27 February the first soldiers reached the deserted summit, and before 4.00 am the whole force had ascended.

Having achieved this considerable coup, Colley and his staff proceeded to fritter it away. The commander was utterly convinced that the summit was impregnable, and remarked to his chief staff officer, Colonel Stewart, 'We could stay here for ever.' It was this fatal misconception that no doubt accounted for Colley's failure to order the immediate construction of entrenchments on the summit itself. This was all the more disastrous because, although to the south-east and the north-west of Majuba's summit precipitous slopes gave the defenders an overwhelming advantage, this was not the case on the northern side which directly faced the Afrikaners at Laing's Nek below. Here a benign grassy slope rolled down towards the enemy, affording him large patches of dead ground where he would be hidden from the defenders on the rim above.

As the dawn broke, however, the British rank and file were exultant and their officers coolly confident. Some men of the 92nd (Highland) Regiment actually began to stand in full view of the Boers below, shaking their fists and savouring their apparent triumph with gusto. Thus by 5 am the Afrikaners knew that the British were on Majuba's summit; the element of surprise was accordingly diluted. But Colley's supreme optimism seemed justified when at about 9 am the enemy began to limber up their ox waggons and gave every sign of being about to withdraw.

Even as the British basked in this news, Commander-General Joubert and the local commander, General Smit, were skilfully preparing to deal them a tremendous blow. Smit detached some 180 crack marksmen to storm Majuba from the north, at the same time a thousand riflemen to keep up a concentrated covering fire from the north and west. It was about 11 o'clock when the storming party moved off.

The British remained blissfully unaware of their peril. The heavy rifle fire was dismissed by Colley's staff as a wanton waste of ammunition, even though here and there a soldier was hit by an enemy bullet. At 1 pm General Colley decided to take a nap;

this was either an indication of a relaxed state of mind or of an unawareness of what was about to happen. Within the hour, however, a great deal had happened.

Though the British defenders of the northern and north-eastern perimeter of Majuba at last realized they were under attack, their freedom of movement was severely restricted by deadly accurate Afrikaner fire. The assault party advanced stealthily, making magnificent use of the hollows of the grassy slope. Suddenly, as if conjured out of the ground, the commandos rose up at two points close to the ridge and shot to pieces a detachment of the Highlanders on the north-western and northern sides of the perimeter. Nearly fifty Scots fell before the survivors gave way and retreated on to the plateau. But the crucial breach had been made. Tragically there was no strong defensive position on the plateau itself. The Boers now isolated small groups of British troops and proceeded to shoot them down. At last an officer (not Colley) gave the order to retreat, and some troops scrambled ignominiously down the steep south-eastern slopes of Majuba while the enemy picked them off.

General Sir George Pomeroy Colley died on the plateau just before the final rout, shot through the head at close range. His death at least spared him from the subsequent flood of recrimination, for he had supervised a series of disastrous reverses culminating in a fully-fledged catastrophe. Of the troops on Majuba's summit 93 were killed, 133 were wounded, and 58 taken prisoner. Boer losses were absurdly small, one man killed and five wounded (one fatally).

Was Colley chiefly to blame for the catastrophe of Majuba Hill? There is no doubt he made scant provision for the defence of the inner plateau, and exhibited an unjustified confidence throughout. He even disregarded three separate reports of the Boer storming party climbing towards the summit. For this there can be no excuse, especially for the officer who had triumphantly left the army's Staff College with 4,274 marks, the biggest total on record and more than 500 ahead of his nearest rival. But his intellectual brilliance was matched with only trifling front-line experience, for even with Wolseley in the Ashanti War he had been in charge of communications and supply. He would have also been wiser to have waited for the arrival of Evelyn Wood and the reinforcements before moving against Majuba Hill.

On the other hand, Colley was pitted against masterful tacticians and born marksmen fighting for their independence. The Boer commandos won the Battle of Majuba Hill just as surely as General Colley lost it. The stealthy progress of the storming party, for instance, gave the British a badly needed lesson in the use of cover. As for marksmanship, two sets of statistics provide a sufficiently telling commentary: only one Boer was killed during the battle; yet of the 93 British dead nearly all were shot above the chest, and of the slaughtered Highlanders a good number had five or six bullets in their heads.

The news of Majuba Hill stunned the British public as much as it exhilarated the Transvaalers. In the British press paeons of mournful praise were written to the unhappy Colley, and the military establishment and many Tories called for speedy revenge. As a youthful midshipman on board HMS *Bacchante* the future King George v delivered his own judgement in a letter to his mother, Princess Alexandra, remarking, 'This is really a dredful war is it not? All these poor people killed & also poor General Colley.'

In the end, the Gladstone government decided to restore independence to the Transvaal, though claiming an ambiguous suzerainty over the restored republic. The confrontation between the British Empire and the Afrikaners of the Transvaal was not, however, over and within two decades a far more titanic struggle broke out. 'Majuba' became a watch-word for both sides: the British were urged to 'Remember Majuba', the Transvaalers celebrated 'Majuba Day'.

Both sides absorbed certain lessons from the war of 1880–81, though not all of them were the right ones. The British gave serious thought to the value of mounted infantry (but did little about it); they also took some pains to improve marksmanship, due partly to the subsequent influence of one of the survivors of

Majuba, Lieutenant (later General Sir Ian) Hamilton, as Commandant of the Musketry School at Hythe; not that the campaign of the Second Boer War of 1899–1902 showed any great improvement in British capabilities in this respect. The Afrikaners emerged from the war of 1880–81 with an understandably low opinion of British military abilities and morale; yet their very triumph led them to underestimate the resilience of the British army if backed to the hilt by a determined government at home; and in October 1899 the Imperial forces in South Africa possessed precisely such support.

Part VI
The Second Boer War
1899–1902

It was our fault, and our very great fault, and *not* the
judgement of Heaven.
We made an Army in our own image, on an island
nine by seven.

Rudyard Kipling, *The Lesson*, 1899–1902.

I not only think blunders have been committed, but I
think they have been of the most serious kind, imperilling the whole progress of the war.... The chief blunders
have been made, in my private opinion, by our Generals
in the field.

Arthur Balfour, January 1900.

15
The March to War

The second South African War broke out in October 1899. Superficially it provided, at the outset at least, a repeat performance of the one act tragedy (or farce) enacted in 1880–81 in the Transvaal. The British Empire was pitted once more against the determined Transvaalers, who were again struggling for their independence; yet again the British army found itself outmanoeuvred, outfought and outwitted; even the leaders of the Transvaal were the same, since Kruger was President and Piet Joubert Commandant-General.

There, however, the comparison ends. The first Boer War saw less than 8,000 Transvaalers defeat a mere 1,000 active British troops; during the second conflict nearly 450,000 men from Britain and her self-governing colonies slowly and relentlessly wore down their 45,000 Afrikaner opponents. The campaign of 1880–81 was over in nine weeks; the war that began in October 1899 lasted for over two and a half years. In 1880 the Transvaal stood alone; in 1899 the Orange Free State also fought for independence, and several thousand Cape Dutch from Cape Colony rallied to the two republics' colours. In 1881 the Transvaal regained its republican status; in 1902 the two Boer republics were annexed by the British Crown. In the first war one inexperienced general, Sir George Colley, led the British forces; in the second war many of the greatest military commanders of the Empire were dispatched to South Africa, among them Sir Redvers Buller, Field-Marshal Lord Roberts of Kandahar, Lord Kitchener of Khartoum, General Sir George White, Lord Methuen and General Sir John French.

Above all the two wars broke out in very different fashions. In 1880 the British government hoped to avoid conflict and were caught by surprise when the Transvaalers rebelled; in 1899 the British Colonial Secretary Joseph Chamberlain, and the Governor of the Cape and High Commissioner for South Africa, Sir Alfred Milner, had decided to push Kruger to the brink of war and, if necessary, over the brink. In 1880 the Transvaalers had argued, in tones of outraged righteousness, that they merely wanted self-government; in 1899 it was the British government that flourished a moral justification for war, arguing that the plight of the Uitlanders in the Transvaal demanded intervention.

The Uitlander problem did not by itself cause war, but it clearly illustrated what the war was about. In 1886 gold was discovered on the Witwatersrand in the Transvaal; within a decade the sleepy dorp of Johannesburg had been transformed into a bustling city of more than 50,000 European inhabitants, and a great gold-mining industry had grown up on the Rand. The Transvaal with its slow, pastoral economy had suddenly spawned a profitable and expanding industrial complex. But the development of the gold-mining industry had only been made possible by British technological skills and financial backing.

The Afrikaners described the British immigrants to the Rand as Uitlanders (foreigners). It was soon reckoned that the Uitlanders outnumbered the Transvaalers. An acute dilemma now faced Kruger's government: the Uitlanders had built up the gold-mining industry and had helped the Transvaal to realize fabulous riches; yet if their request for full civil rights, especially the franchise, were to be granted, then the Transvaal might well have an English-speaking administration. If this bloodless revolution should take place it would fly in the face of sixty years of Afrikaner determination to avoid British rule; all the heroic exertions of earlier years, from the Great Trek to the war of 1880–81, would have been rendered useless by a few hundred ballot boxes stuffed with Uitlander votes.

Kruger was therefore understandably reluctant to enfranchise the Uitlanders, though some were in fact allowed the vote. In turn, the British government, especially after the Conservative and Unionist election victory in 1895, supported the claims of its citizens in the Transvaal. There were, of course, other and deeper reasons to seek a show-down with Kruger's Republic: chief among these was the fear that instead of a South African federation eventually taking place under the leadership of the British self-governing colony of the Cape, it was increasingly likely that the expanding economy of the Transvaal would guarantee it a dominant position in southern Africa; any federation would therefore grow up under the *vierkleur* not the Union Jack.

Given the huge economic potential of South Africa, there were influential voices raised against the Transvaal's government. In December 1895 Cecil Rhodes, diamond and gold millionaire, and dreamer of dreams of Imperial expansion, tried to overthrow Kruger's Republic by an armed raid from Bechuanaland. But the raid led by Dr Jameson, Rhodes's friend and lieutenant from his Kimberley mining days, was a flop. The Uitlanders of Johannesburg were meant to rise in rebellion and link up with Jameson's troopers of the Rhodesian-based British South African police force – but they failed to do so. Jameson and his men were rounded up by Boer commandos and handed over to the British authorities for trial. Rhodes was forced to resign as Prime Minister of the Cape, and British policy in South Africa had suffered a tremendous set-back.

But within four years, Joseph Chamberlain, Colonial Secretary from 1895–1903, had regained the initiative. He had stripped the Transvaal of foreign (mainly German) diplomatic support; he had appointed the determined race-patriot Sir Alfred Milner to the Governorship of the Cape in 1897, and within a year Milner had come to the conclusion that war with the Transvaal was inevitable; he had also partly salvaged his reputation from the accusations of complicity in the Jameson Raid.

Above all, Chamberlain had manoeuvred Britain into an extremely favourable diplomatic position by the late summer of 1899 : British public opinion had been prepared for a war to 'free' the Uitlanders; Kruger had made apparently inadequate concessions regarding the Uitlander franchise at the Bloemfontein Conference of May 1899; the Sudan war was drawing to a brilliant and successful close. Finally, in October 1899, the presence of British troops on the Transvaal's borders provoked an ultimatum, demanding their withdrawal, from the Transvaal, backed by the Orange Free State; the ultimatum was ignored and Britain could thus conveniently pose as the outraged party in a war which was in essence of her own choosing.

British military preparations for the war reflected Chamberlain's and Milner's determination to push Kruger into hostilities if necessary. As early as June 1899 the Colonial Secretary and the Governor of the Cape were discussing the question of troop reinforcements. During August there were further warlike preparations. By the beginning of October there were nearly 20,000 Imperial troops in the Cape and Natal, and when fighting broke out on 12 October there were 70,000 British soldiers either in South Africa or on the high seas.

But the dispatch of an army corps of 50,000 revealed serious inadequacies in the British military establishment. For one thing, home defences had to be pared to the bone; so serious was the depletion of forces stationed in Britain that the War Office immediately pressed the Cabinet to approve a policy of 'replacement', which involved the embodiment of a number of militia battalions and the issuing of contracts for new uniforms and supplies. George Wyndham, Under Secretary at the War Office, told

Arthur Balfour, the First Lord of the Treasury, in October 1899, that unless 'replacement' was speedily effected the home army would be left without 'personnel and material' for adequate action or for training recruits, there would only be eight cavalry regiments left in the United Kingdom (not enough for home defence or for supplying the Indian army in the coming year), and that 'we are left with nothing but four gun batteries'.

None of this was evident to the British public, many of whom revelled in the exhilarating atmosphere of mobilization and dispatch. As the khaki-clad infantry marched to the troopships, as the Admiralty hastily mustered 600,000 tons of shipping for the men, horses, guns and supplies of the Army Corps, as General Sir Redvers Buller left Waterloo station for embarkation at Southampton and the command of Her Majesty's forces in South Africa, it was Rudyard Kipling who caught the current mood when he wrote :

> He's an absent minded beggar, and his weaknesses are great
> But we and Paul must take him as we find him –
> He is out on active service, wiping something off a slate –
> And he's left a lot of little things behind him !
> Duke's son – cook's son – son of a hundred kings
> (Fifty thousand horse and foot going to Table Bay !)

In the Transvaal and the Free State equally frenzied preparations were taking place. Commando units were speedily mobilized, and a Free Stater, Victor Pohl, later recalled the mustering of one typical force :

> Soon there were gathered a large number of farmer-soldiers, hefty, clear-eyed, bronzed, and good-natured men from the open veld. . . . Sitting their horses like cowboys, they wore what they had stood up in when they were called up, and their rifles and bandoliers were slung carelessly on their persons according to individual inclination. A raincoat or blanket, or both, were rolled tightly

and fastened to the pommel or tail of each saddle, and in most cases saddle-bags stuffed to bursting with boer-rusks, bread, and biltong (dried meat), completed their outfits. To an outsider this motley and unwarlike gathering would have appeared to be without leaders or discipline, for the Boer leaders did not differ in appearance from the rest of the slouching burghers. And yet when they addressed the men they were listened to with earnest attention, although not with parade-ground rigidity. What these men lacked in military discipline was largely made up for by their independence of thought and action, and their sense of responsibility. Moreover many of the men were deeply religious, and all these qualities, combined with their profound faith in their cause, their reliance on themselves and their Mausers, and the knowledge that they were fighting for their homes and country, made of this undisciplined crowd a formidable army, one to whose prowess the civilized world was to pay tribute.

The Afrikaner forces boasted few regular troops: there were less than 2,000 men drawn from various police detachments, and a few hundred artillerymen from the Transvaal's Staatsartillerie and from the Free State's artillery corps, which was Prussian-trained and even wore Prussian helmets. Their guns were excellent – from the 94-pounder 'Long Toms' to the one-pounder Vickers-Maxim pom poms, and the 75mm Krupp and Creusot quick-firing field pieces. In all, however, they possessed no more than 70 guns, whereas the British forces eventually built up a vast preponderance in artillery and could count on a thousand fifteen-pounders alone, as well as on nearly a thousand machine guns.

Of course, the crucial test came when both sides handled their artillery. Here the Boers often showed greater ingenuity and skill. When they opened up at the siege of Ladysmith with their 'Long Toms', Joseph Chamberlain remarked irritably that Lord Lansdowne, Secretary of State for War had told him 'that modern guns require elaborate platforms and mountings which took a year to consolidate. The Boers apparently find no difficulty in working their "Long Toms" without these elaborate precautions. On the whole I am terribly afraid that our War Office is as inefficient as usual.'

Much the same comparisons can be made between the small arms used by both sides. The Afrikaners were mostly equipped with the clip-loading Mauser rifle; the British carried the Lee-Metford rifle whose magazine had to be loaded round by round. Neither rifle was obviously superior in range to the other, but given Afrikaner marksmanship and expertise, the Mauser, with its quick loading action, was generally employed far more effectively than the Lee-Metford.

The British forces had hardly profited from their humiliations during the brief war of 1880–81. The average infantryman was still expected to obey rigid instructions to the last syllable, to keep splendid order, and to let his superiors do the thinking for him, whereas each Afrikaner was his own general. The British army possessed no General Staff to plan and coordinate tactics and strategy, and a paltry £11,000 was spent per annum on maintaining the Intelligence Division. The 'ideal British battle' was still one like the engagement at Omdurman in 1898, when the spear-waving Dervishes of the Sudan ran in their thousands against their opponents' maxim guns and rifles and were annihilated; Kitchener, the victor of Omdurman, was later to complain in South Africa that the Boers would not 'stand up to a fair fight'.

Nor had the British army properly understood the importance of mounted infantry. Although at the outset ten per cent of the Imperial troops were mounted, they were mainly cavalry who, although they carried the new-fangled carbines as well as sabres and lances, remained cavalrymen – not mounted infantry. The authorities were soon scouring the Empire for mounted men. Happily the self-governing colonies were able to plug an important gap or two: 1,000 expert horsemen were raised in Canada, the New South Wales Lancers played a conspicuous part in the war, and from southern Africa itself came the Imperial Light Horse (mostly recruited from the Uitlanders of Johannesburg), the Natal Mounted Volunteers, the Cape Police, the Kimberley Light Horse, and several other units.

These valuable contributions were only part of the generous colonial response to the war, and eventually 55,000 men, mostly from the self-governing parts of the Empire, served in South Africa – nearly double the number of the British expeditionary force sent to the Crimea in 1854. Even so, the bulk of the colonial troops did not arrive until the war was well under way, and it was not until the beginning of 1901 that Lord Kitchener managed to assemble sufficiently large numbers of mounted men to try to cope with Boer mobility. But despite the 80,000 mounted troops under British command by 1901, their quality remained variable, and few units could match the Afrikaners in versatility and guile.

In the exultant early days of the war, however, few British patriots doubted that the conflict would be speedily ended. A popular marching song 'Goodbye Dolly Gray' swept the music halls, and seemed merely a brash overture to inevitable military conquest. And there was unbounded public confidence in the Commander in Chief, General Buller: 'farver' said the urchin in the cartoon ' 'as gawn to South Africa, and tooken 'is strap!'

But Buller's real capacities fell far short of appearances. Come to that, even Dolly Gray was a second-hand trollop who had waved American troops off to the war against Spain the year before! Buller's failings, however, were to prove rather more serious. He was sixty years old in 1899: over-weight, ponderous and self-indulgent; he later boasted that he consumed a pint of good champagne every day during his campaigning in South Africa – and there was certainly a good deal of evidence that his judgement had been impaired by heavy drinking. Equally serious, though unavoidable, was his complete lack of experience against European opponents; when he left for South Africa he had never commanded more than 2,000 men at once, and even then against a variety of poorly-armed indigenous people. He was undoubtedly brave, and had won the Victoria Cross at Hlobane during the Zulu War; he also took remarkable care of his soldier's welfare. Yet beneath the surface glitter he was painfully unsure of himself, and was soon to reveal considerable prowess as a military fumbler and ditherer, thus amply justifying a brother officer's description of him as 'a superb Major, a mediocre Colonel and an abysmally poor General'.

Still, there seemed at the outset no reason why Buller and the Army Corps that were descending upon South Africa should not achieve prompt victory. The British forces would move north along the railway lines from Port Elizabeth, Cape Town and East London, and would eventually sweep on to the Afrikaner capitals of Bloemfontein in the Orange Free State, and Pretoria in the Transvaal. The plan seemed perfectly adequate, and as the *Dunottar Castle*, with Buller and his staff aboard, left Southampton there seemed every justification for the enthusiasm of a big, red-faced onlooker who repeatedly shouted 'Remember Majuba!' 'He need not have worried', a member of Buller's staff was later to recall, 'we soon had plenty of Majubas of our own.'

16
From 'Black Week' to Spion Kop

Even as Buller steamed towards the Cape, British fortunes in South Africa were suffering sharp reverses. Far from waiting like bemused rabbits to be devoured by their ponderous enemies, the Boers immediately struck against Cape Colony and Natal. Three Afrikaner columns invaded Natal: Utrecht and Newcastle were occupied, and soon Ladysmith, on the junction of the railway lines between Natal, the Free State and the Transvaal, was under siege. Meanwhile, further west, Afrikaner troops infested two more towns that lay on the vital railway line that ran from the important junction at De Aar, in the Cape, roughly parallel with the western borders of the Free State and the Transvaal until it finally entered the British protectorate of Bechuanaland. The names of these two towns, Kimberley and Mafeking, together with Ladysmith, were about to become world famous. To the south of the Free State's border with Cape Colony, Boer columns also pushed towards the railway junction of Stormberg and towards the rail link between Naauwpoort and De Aar.

At the end of November, British forces under Generals Gatacre and French moved against this invasion of the potentially rebellious northern Cape; in Natal, Buller established a huge base camp at Frere, twenty-five miles south of Ladysmith, where he mustered nearly 20,000 amply equipped men; at the painfully-gained Modder River station, some twenty-seven miles to the south of Kimberley, Lord Methuen was preparing to lead 13,000 men to the relief of the besieged diamond capital. During a single week in December, however, these three British offensives were each to suffer such serious rebuffs that the nation was finally shocked out of its lazy assumption that the war could be won quite easily and cheaply.

The disasters of 'Black Week' began with the Battle of Stormberg on 10 December. On 9 December the gaunt, energetic General Gatacre (known to his troops as 'General Backacher') ordered 3,000 men on to the train for Molteno, the nearest friendly station before Stormberg Junction. About 2,300 Boers, led by General Olivier, defended the pass that led to Stormberg. Gatacre was an over-enthusiastic exponent of the night march and the dawn attack, perhaps cherishing the illusion that he could thus bring off a coup as spectacular as Garnet Wolseley's celebrated victory at Tel-el Kebir during the 1882 invasion of Egypt. On this occasion, however, things went badly wrong.

Although Gatacre's men were up at 4 am on 9 December, due to bungled transport arrangements the entire force did not reach Molteno until 8.30 in the evening. It was not until 9.15 pm that men of the Irish Rifles and the Northumberland Fusiliers moved out of Molteno towards Stormberg Junction. Gatacre had decided that it was foolhardy to push on down the main pass, and instead planned to take the western end of a range of Kopjes called the Kissieberg, from which he could dominate the route into Stormberg.

Unfortunately the one guide who knew the terrain well had been left behind, and Gatacre had to rely on guides who were soon lost and, worse still, refused to admit it. With bayonets fixed, the men stumbled on through the darkness; they had by now been without sleep for twenty-four hours, and were soon to fight a well-rested enemy. As dawn broke the British force was actually *behind* the Kissieberg and moving in the wrong direction, whereas Gatacre believed that they were in front of it and about to advance into the railway pass!

Boer pickets on the eastern end of the Kissieberg suddenly saw the British beneath them. They gave the alarm and their comrades opened fire. Bereft of clear orders the British infantry hurled themselves heroically at the steep slopes of the hills; a few scrambled to the top of the range where they were dispersed by misdirected fire from their own artillery. In half an hour it was all over, and most of the battered and disorganized troops, fired on from two sides, were making an undignified retreat to Molteno. But 600 men of the Northumberland Fusiliers had received no orders to withdraw and were left behind on the Kissieberg. Most of these were forced to surrender to the Afrikaners, which meant that, together with the ninety-odd battle casualties, the British lost nearly 700 troops at Stormberg, and the junction remained in enemy hands. So inexplicable did this reverse seem to the authorities in London, that the news of the disaster, published on 11 December, claimed that Gatacre had been led into an ambush by treacherous guides!

On the same day that Gatacre's drive on Stormberg distintegrated, Lord Methuen was preparing to march on Kimberley, where an irate and jumpy Cecil Rhodes was at odds with the garrison commander, Colonel Kekewich, and inveighing against military men in general. Between Methuen and Kimberley lay the Magersfontein hills, dominated on the right by Magersfontein Hill itself, upon whose slopes the Boers were entrenched. Methuen decided that the best way to carry Magersfontein Hill, and thus to open the way to Kimberley, was by an artillery bombardment followed by a dawn assault headed by the redoubtable Highland Brigade.

On Sunday 10 December, Methuen's guns opened up on Magersfontein; the hill rocked under its one and a half hour's pounding, and it seemed certain to British observers that the Boer entrenchments must be shattered and the enemy dispersed. But ironically the vast bulk of Piet Cronje's force of 8,500 men were not on Magersfontein at all. They were concealed in a long line of narrow trenches running along the foot of Magersfontein and almost to the Modder river twelve miles away. The decision to forsake the traditional protection of the hills had been taken against Cronje's advice when the Free State's President Steyn had backed Kooss de la Rey's plan to entrench an extended position on the plain at the base of Magersfontein hill.

The result of this tactical innovation was that the British walked straight into a devastating ambush. In the early hours of 11 December the Highland Brigade, composed of the Seaforths, the Gordons, the Argylls, the Black Watch and the Highland Light Infantry, moved off towards Magersfontein. Despite a violent storm overhead, and tacky going underfoot, the High-landers had got to within half a mile of Magersfontein by 4 am. Their commander, Major General Andy Wauchope ordered them to extend their line prior to the assault. But as the 4,000 men began to spread out, a murderous fusilade from the Boer trenches cut them to pieces. Within seconds hundreds were killed or wounded, and General Wauchope lay dead. Amazingly about a hundred Highlanders pressed on, broke through the trenches, and began climbing Magersfontein. But by an extraordinary coincidence, Piet Cronje and six of his adjutants, who had lost their way while reconnoitring, wandered into their path and blazed away at them until reinforcements sealed the gap in the Boer entrenchments.

As the sun rose, the Afrikaners saw hundreds of the Highland Brigade lying face downwards on the sandy plain not daring to move. Despite a suicidal attempt by some men to rush the enemy's trenches, and a fitful skirl or two of the bagpipes, the majority of the survivors sweated it out in the scorching heat until at about 1.30 pm their morale understandably crumbled and they rose and escaped as best they could. Night fell with hundreds of wounded still lying unattended before the trenches.

The next day, 12 December, Methuen decided to order a

general withdrawal, after an armistice had allowed both sides to deal with their wounded and dead. The Boers, as so often in this war, were disinclined or unable to mercilessly harry the retreating British troops. By 4 pm the shattered force was back at its camp on the Modder River. Their losses were 210 killed and 738 wounded; among the dead were Wauchope, and the Marquis of Winchester; the leading companies of the Highland Brigade lost 60 per cent of their officers. The Afrikaners suffered comparatively trifling losses with eighty-seven killed and 188 wounded; Methuen's devastating bombardment of Magersfontein hill had merely wounded three of the enemy.

Methuen must bear criticism for his generalship at Magersfontein. He set too much store on night marches and dawn attacks, which were potentially risky and apt to exhaust the troops. He had no knowledge of the real Boer positions, and too few cavalry to reconnoitre properly. It is also arguable that he withdrew too soon, since his other brigades (including the Guards) were hardly thrown into the battle and might even have turned the Afrikaner flank.

Even as Methuen fell back on to the Modder river, General Buller with an army of 18,000 was setting out to dislodge 8,000 men under General Louis Botha from Colenso where the railway and road to Ladysmith crossed the Tugela. The Boers were apprehensive at the coming battle, not merely because they were heavily outnumbered but also because of Buller's martial reputation. They need not have worried : Botha was a commander of supreme gifts, and Buller was about to reveal his inadequacies for all to see.

Sir George White, the beleaguered commander of Ladysmith, was expecting to coordinate with Buller's attack on Colenso by dispatching a sizeable field force against his Afrikaner besiegers. Unfortunately Buller failed to inform him of the date of his own attack, and the first that White knew of it was the rumble of guns across the Tugela. For two days Buller's artillery pounded Botha's positions. But the Boers gave nothing away; they did not budge, and their exact whereabouts remained a mystery to the British.

At dawn on 17 December Buller's men moved towards the Tugela. At the front Colonel Long forged ahead with twelve field pieces and six naval guns under his command. But within two hundred yards of the river the concealed Boers poured a withering fire into the field piece batteries. In under an hour scores of men had fallen, including the foolhardy Long, who shouted, though seriously wounded, 'Abandon be damned! We never abandon guns!' But the twelve field pieces could be defended no longer, and they were left useless and marooned on the banks of the Tugela.

Meanwhile, on the left flank, Major-General Hart muffed an attack with his Irish Brigade. A firm believer in strict discipline and close, parade-ground, order, Hart rashly led his unfortunate troops into the northern loop of the river where Botha's men were presented with a glorious target. The Irish Brigade was soon immobilized by heavy fire. British fortunes were no better on the right flank where detachments of the Mounted Brigade made an unsuccessful attack on Hlangwhane, a hill that dominated Colenso to the west.

Buller, who had sat impassively watching these abortive assaults, munching some sandwiches, at last decided to withdraw. Dismayed that he had lost so many of his guns, he ordered a desperate rescue attempt which in fact succeeded in dragging two of the field-pieces clear, though at the cost of several lives. Among those mortally wounded was Captain the Honourable F.H.S. Roberts, only son of Field-Marshal Lord Roberts of Kandahar. By a painful irony, Buller's indecisive tactics at Colenso not only contributed, indirectly, to Captain Robert's death but also to the home government's decision to supersede him as Commander-in-Chief in South Africa with the bereaved Lord Roberts.

But Captain Roberts was not the only casualty at Colenso. The British lost 143 killed and 1,002 wounded. Botha's men lost a mere seven killed and twenty-two wounded, a result of their well-entrenched positions and also of the smokeless powder used to fire their Mauser rifles which made their location difficult to assess.

The three disasters of 'Black Week' stunned the British public.

There was a dichotomous response: on the one hand, patriots thumped the Imperial drum with renewed, even hysterical, vigour; on the other, a mounting volume of criticism was directed against the conduct of the war, and even against the justice of the British cause. In January 1900 Arthur Balfour, the First Lord of the Treasury, delivered himself of the private opinion in a letter to his brother-in-law, Henry Sidgwick, that 'I not only think blunders have been committed, but I think they have been of the most serious kind, imperilling the whole progress of the war. . . . The chief blunders had been made . . . by our Generals in the field.' *Punch* magazine tried to extract some wry humour from the enforced immobility of the British forces when it announced 'Nigger News from Transvaal: De British hab got alongside o' Modder. But they habn't got no Farder.'

For Private Thomas Atkins, who was supposed to be 'wiping something off a slate', there was little to laugh at. Earl de la Warr, on active service in South Africa, thought that the common soldier's lot in the campaign was a far from happy one:

> Modder River, South Africa, December 25th. The battles in this campaign do not consist of a few hours' fighting, then a grand charge, resulting in the rout of the enemy, when men can see the effect of their work. No; this is very different. Think of it, a two-mile march under the fire of an invisible foe, then perhaps eight or ten hours' crouching behind any available cover – an ant hill or a scrubby bush – when the slightest movement on a man's part at once enables the hidden enemy to put him out of action, whereas he never has a chance of retaliating. Certainly this is fighting in circumstances which require extraordinarily good nerve and courage. And when the day is over 'Tommy' has not even had the satisfaction of knowing what he has accomplished. When the day comes which will give him an opportunity of getting at close quarters with the Boer, he will remember the long and weary hours he has spent facing the enemy's trenches.

Little of this chastened mood had yet percolated to those robust domestic patriots who were simultaneously revelling in the mawkish sentiment surrounding the story of the fourteen-year-old bugler, John Dunne, who lost his bugle in the Tugela at the Battle of Colenso. Queen Victoria gave him a new bugle at Osborne, and the incident was preserved for a more cynical posterity in a popular verse :

What shall we give, my little Bugelar,
What for the bugle you lost at Tugelar?
Give me another! that I may go
To the front and return them blow for blow.

The burden of revenge for the fiasco at Colenso, however, for the moment rested squarely on the heavy shoulders of General Buller. Although superseded at the end of December 1899 as Commander-in-Chief in South Africa by Lord Roberts, with Kitchener as his second-in-command, Buller was preparing another drive to relieve Ladysmith. He now had 30,000 men with the addition of a new division under General Sir Charles Warren. On 16 January 1900, Buller set off with 24,000 infantry, 2,500 mounted troops, eight field batteries and ten naval guns, planning to cross the Tugela at Trickhardt's Drift and 'gain the open plain north of Spion Kop'. To do this he proposed to send Warren's division on a sweeping left flanking movement round the Rangeworthy Hills then on eastwards to the town of Dewdrop where it would link up with General Lyttelton's Brigade forging up from the south over Potgeiter's Drift. The Boers' hill entrenchments would thus have been turned, and the combined columns could press on to Ladysmith fifteen miles away.

At first the advance went well. The Tugela was efficiently bridged and the troops and their bountiful supplies taken across in excellent order. Lord Dundonald's cavalry moved in a great leftwards arc towards Acton Homes on the road to Ladysmith. To their rear, General Warren found the route too difficult for his wagons; he therefore halted at Fairview at the foot of the Rangeworthy Hills. Calling back Dundonald's cavalry, he now proposed to dislodge the Boers by a direct attack on the hills. Surveying the terrain he decided to occupy the highest peak on the ridge – Spion Kop. From this vantage point he could then enfilade the Afrikaner trenches and dominate the Fairview-Rosalie road to Ladysmith.

After obtaining grudging approval from Buller for his assault on Spion Kop, General Warren divided his force into a Left Attack and a Right Attack. The latter group, under Major-General Coke, were chosen to seize Spion Kop, though Lieutenant-Colonel Thorneycroft, who had sketched out the landmarks on the route up the mountain, actually acted as guide. The assault column set off before midnight, and grappled in the mist with the steep, rock-strewn slope of Spion Kop, fearing detection at any moment. But in fact the men managed to attain the summit before a Boer picket challenged them. Even so the troops were able to dislodge seventy or so Afrikaners with a brisk bayonet charge, and at 4 am on 26 January Spion Kop was in British hands.

For three hours, while the mist hung over the summit, the troops dug themselves in. But the hard ground prevented the construction of anything more than a dangerously shallow entrenchment with a parapet. Then, at about 7 am, the mist began to lift, revealing the true situation. The British had won only part of the summit. Worse still, their entrenchments were pitifully exposed to enemy fire from all directions; field guns, pom poms and rifles could be directed at the British positions. Within an hour the Lancashire Fusiliers, the Scottish Rifles and General Thorneycroft's Mounted Infantry were being systematically slaughtered. The Lancashire Fusiliers were caught in a terrible enfilade fire from the Twin Peaks to the east, and soon their shallow trench was piled high with bodies. The surviving Lancashires began waving white handkerchiefs, or trying to slip off down the hill. The redoubtable Thorneycroft, reinforced by men of the Middlesex Regiment and the Imperial Light Infantry, managed, however, to retrieve the situation on the summit and, with further assistance from the Scottish Rifles, held the hill top for the rest of the day.

Bad though the British position on Spion Kop had proved to be, it was made worse by Buller's generalship. There was great confusion as to who was in command at the summit: General Woodgate, the brigade commander, was severely wounded, and Buller at last told General Warren to put Thorneycroft in charge; but Major-General Coke, the officer commanding the Right Attack, and Lieutenant-Colonel Hill of the Middlesex Regiment, were mysteriously not informed of this crucial decision. More serious still was Buller's reaction to the success of General Lyttleton's Brigade, which had crossed the Tugela at Potgeiter's Drift and then stormed the Twin Peaks, east of Spion Kop and the source of some of the most destructive enfilading fire. Lyttleton's triumph on the Twin Peaks, alas, was not in accordance with Buller's overall plan, and at sunset the troop was recalled. A real chance of averting defeat was thus cast away.

Night fell with Thorneycroft still holding on to the summit. But when the young war correspondent Winston Churchill managed to reach Thorneycroft in the darkness with messages from Warren, he found that the summit commander had decided to withdraw. Churchill was shocked at the sight of the exhausted, wounded and dead troops on Spion Kop, and appreciated Thorneycroft's conviction that he had been sacrificed to the incompetence of his superiors who had allowed thousands of fresh troops to stand idly by while he and his men had struggled for survival.

But even as Thorneycroft's men were staggering down from the summit, the Boers were similarly drifting away from Spion Kop. An earlier assault on the British position by nearly 900 of the enemy had been beaten back; and Lyttleton's temporary occupation of the Twin Peaks was an ominous challenge. At about 2 am, however, the tireless efforts of Louis Botha halted the Boer dispersal. As the Afrikaners reluctantly returned to the foot of Spion Kop some of them saw in the breaking dawn two men on the summit waving their hats in triumph; they had scaled the hill and found it deserted.

The British had withdrawn first, thus handing victory to their opponents. Buller had insisted on a complete retreat across the Tugela, which he supervised with his characteristic care. But he had lost 1,750 men killed, wounded and captured on Spion Kop, while the Boers had lost a mere 300. Moreover, Ladysmith was not relieved.

Spion Kop was a British defeat partly because both Buller and Warren stuck to plans which Dundonald's cavalry dash towards Acton Homes and Lyttleton's occupation of the Twin Peaks ought to have been allowed to amend; there were also appalling communications between the senior officers involved; nor did the British, once Thorneycroft had accepted defeat, have anyone of the calibre of Botha to rally their men for one last effort.

The news of the 'sickening fiasco' as Joseph Chamberlain called it outraged and depressed the British public. Accusations of muddle and incompetence multiplied. Buller received a new, and unkindly nickname, 'the Ferryman of the Tugela'; Lloyd George and the 'pro-Boers' redoubled their criticism of the war; and the great powers of Europe took further delight in British discomfiture. As for Buller, he plodded on a little more, surprisingly secure in his troops' affection, but knowing that the direction of the war was about to be placed in hands more competent than his own.

17
Epilogue: An Inglorious Victory

Field-Marshal Roberts and Lord Kitchener promptly reversed the trend of the war. At the end of February 1900 the main Afrikaner army was soundly defeated at Paardeberg; a few days earlier Kimberley was relieved, and on the last day of the month the 118-day siege of Ladysmith was ended. On 17 May Mafeking, too, was relieved and the British cities, especially London, were thronged with exuberant patriots celebrating the town's deliverance after a siege of 217 days. On 5 June, having previously entered Johannesburg, Lord Roberts marched into the Transvaal's capital of Pretoria. The Union Jack flew once more over the town which the British had abandoned in 1881; it also flew for the first time in Bloemfontein, the Orange Free State's capital.

The three besieged towns had attracted a colossal amount of attention in Britain, as if their fate and the fate of the British Empire hung equally in the balance. Of course, their defenders had suffered considerable hardship and deprivation. Baden-

M

Powell, the hero of Mafeking, described the measures taken to utilize every available source of supply :

> When a horse was killed, his mane and tail were cut off and sent to the hospital for stuffing mattresses and pillows. His shoes went to the foundry for making shells. His skin after having the hair scalded off, was boiled with his head and feet for many hours, chopped up small, and ... served out as 'brawn'.
>
> His flesh was taken from the bones and minced in a great mincing machine and from his inside were made skins into which the meat was crammed and each man received a sausage as his ration.
>
> The bones were then boiled into rich soup, which was dealt out at the different soup kitchens; and they were afterwards pounded into powder with which to adulterate the flour.

But the hazards and deprivations of the besieged garrisons were essentially small scale, and the besiegers behaved in a generally humane, even unbusinesslike, fashion. Colonel Mapleton, who was Principal Medical officer in Ladysmith, gave a revealing account of conditions there in several letters :

> We are besieged by a large force of Boers, and although we have 10,000 men here we can't get out and so are waiting until we are relieved. We had about three very hot days in Ladysmith as the Boers shelled the town and the shells were screaming and bursting all over the place and considering the number of shells very few people were hit though there were many narrow escapes. I had no particular near-shave myself but one lump of shell about six by four inches fell pretty close to me and nearer to where I had passed. Such a lot of shells fell into and about the hospital that on the representation of Sir George White to Joubert, all the hospitals moved out to a bit of neutral ground four miles from the town and here we are now. We are close to the enemy position and can see them with the naked eye. I think we are all glad to get out of here for

the shell-fire was too hot to be pleasant and someone must have been hit if we had stayed where we were.

I have seen some of the Boers for as I am in charge of the hospital out here, I have several times met the Boers under a flag of truce to discuss sundry matters. Those I have seen have all been very pleasant fellows indeed and very friendly. They have behaved extremely well to our wounded prisoners, attending to them and giving them everything they had themselves. All our wounded speak highly of the kindness they have received at their hands. . . .

The bullet the Boers use is an extraordinary missile : it is about one and a quarter inches long and as thin as a lead pencil. It incapacitates a man but it does not kill him like the old Martini and other bullets. I have seen men shot through the brain, matter oozing out of the hole in the skull and yet the man recovered very shortly too. Men shot through the lungs have very little trouble from the wounds. If it catches a hard bone it at times smashes it, but generally drills a hole right through it. The shell wounds are of course ghastly to a degree. . . .

The shops are all shut in Ladysmith, and some of the civil population have been cleared out into this camp which is a very big one. . . . We get lots to eat though I dare say you would turn up your snout at it, for the quality though all right for camp is not what one would select for choice, still besieged people have to be thankful for what they can get. The water is like pea soup but we boil it and filter it.

A good deal of big gun firing goes on all day, and now and again the Boers let off all their guns into the town at midnight – no one knows why. They have knocked down a lot of houses in Ladysmith but have done comparatively little damage. Two of our officers were sitting side by side having lunch at the hotel; a shell burst just outside the house, and a big lump of it came through the window and actually went between them as they sat, and hurt no one. Pretty close shave that ! One shell came into our camp, but did not burst, but rolled through the camp and through a tent and hurt no one. Many shells have burst close to people and not hurt them. One burst in a room in which were thirteen people, and no one was hurt. Of course there is a reverse side of the picture.

I get about fifty-five sick a day into this hospital, and I am now in charge of no less than 1,270 sick and wounded, including sixty-five officers. I have a very insufficient staff of both officers and men to do the enormous amount of work: about 500 cases of enteric fever, 180 of dysentery and 150 wounded.

Not all British onlookers indulged in crass exultation when the besieged towns were relieved. There were, for example, critics who remained astonished that Sir George White had immediately retreated with 10,000 men into Ladysmith at the outset of the Natal campaign. Writing in May 1900 from South Africa, Violet Cecil told her influential cousin Arthur Balfour:

I hear at home none of you care a brass button about Army Reform. I wish you could come to South Africa for a fortnight to be converted. . . . I see you are all making a fuss about Ladysmith – it was a miserable performance, and the fuss is like nothing but the fuss made by the French after the Madagascar Campaign which we all laughed at. Oh Arthur, please don't praise the things which are not worth it, it makes everything so disheartening.

Still the war seemed over by June 1900, yet in fact it had still nearly two years to run. About 20,000 Boer commandos fought on. They were led by men of consummate military skills, whose names were soon to become household words throughout the world – Botha, Smuts, de Wet, de la Rey, Hertzog and many more. To combat these elusive enemies the British applied tactics which were, in essence, an admission of failure. Kitchener supervised the longest and harshest period of the drive against the commandos from December 1900 (when he succeeded Roberts as

Commander-in-Chief) until the Peace of Vereeniging in May 1902.

One technique of 'Kitchener's War' was farm-burning. This had started even before Roberts left South Africa for honour and acclaim at home, and between June and November 1900 more than 600 Afrikaner farms were burnt in the Free State alone. The object of farm-burning was to deny the commandos vital supplies from the Afrikaner civilian population. This scorched-earth policy had a limited success, as General Christian de Wet later admitted in his book *Three Years' War*:

> I had to wait there [near Heilbron] till the evening of 31 December until the necessary waggons and oxen had been got together for carrying the ammunition with us. Waggons were now no longer easily to be got, because the British had not only taken them away from the farms but had also burnt many of them ... even where there were waggons the women had always to keep them in readiness to fly in them before the columns of the enemy, who had now already command to carry the women away from their dwellings to the concentration camps – which the British called Refugee Camps. Proclamations had been issued by Lord Roberts, prescribing that any building within ten miles of the railway, where the Boers had blown up the railway line should be burnt down.

De Wet's mention of concentration camps is a significant one. Mainly to house the Boer women, children and aged men who had been made homeless by the farm-burning campaign the British authorities set up forty-six camps in which these refugees were 'concentrated' under supervision. Farm-burning and the rounding up of civilians quickly caused adverse comment from liberal and moderate opinion at home, and many of the soldiers who carried out the policy probably had feelings as mixed as those described by Captain R.F. Talbot of the Royal Horse Artillery in his diary for 1901:

> I went out this morning with some of my men ostensibly to get vegetables, but joined the provost marshal and the

sappers in a farm burning party, and we burnt and blew up two farms with gun-cotton, turning out the inhabitants first. It is a bit sickening at first turning out the women and children, but they are such brutes and the former all spies; we don't mind it now. Only those are done which belong to men who are sniping or otherwise behaving badly.

By October 1901, however, overcrowded and insanitary conditions in the concentration camps were causing an average annual death-rate of 344 per thousand. Due in great measure to the persistent agitation of Emily Hobhouse, women's Secretary of the South Africa Conciliation Committee, ('that bloody woman' as Kitchener described her) conditions were drastically improved, and by the end of the war the death-rate was down to 69 per thousand. But more than 20,000 concentration camp inmates died before the Peace of Vereeniging, a bitter legacy for the ensuing era of reconstruction and reconciliation.

Early in 1901 Kitchener further attempted to counter commando mobility with an enormous network of block-houses and barbed-wire fences stretching for hundreds of miles over the open veld. Formidable though these barriers seemed, the Boer commandos were adept at slipping through them. De Wet had no high opinion of them, and subsequently wrote :

On my return I learnt that the enemy were occupied in building a line of blockhouses from Heilbron to Frankfort (in the north-east of the Free State). It had always seemed to me a most unaccountable circumstance that England – the all-powerful – could not catch the Boers without the aid of these blockhouses. . . . Still narrower and narrower did the circle become, hemming us in more closely at every moment. The result was that they 'bagged' an enormous number of men and cattle, without a solitary burgher or, for the matter of that, a solitary ox, having been captured by means of their famous block-house system. The English have been constantly boasting in the newspapers about the advantages of their blockhouses; but they have never been able to give an instance of a capture effected by them. On the contrary, when during the later stages of the war, it happened, as it often did, that they drove some of our men against one or other of the great blockhouse lines which then intersected the country, and it became necessary for us to fight our way through, we generally succeeded in doing so.... There were thousands of miles of blockhouse lines which made a sort of spider's web of the South African Republics. The blockhouses themselves were sometimes round, sometimes angled erections. The roofs were always of iron. The walls were pierced with loop-holes four feet from the ground, and from four to six feet from each other. Between the blockhouses were fences, made with five strands of barbed-wire. Parallel with these was a trench, three feet deep and four to five feet across the top, but narrower at the bottom. Where the material could be procured, there was also a stone wall to serve as an additional obstacle. Sometimes there were two lines of fences, the upper one – erected on top of the earth thrown up from the trench – consisting of three or four strands only. There was thus a regular network of wires in the vicinity of the blockhouses – the English seemed to think that a Boer might be netted like a fish.

The 20,000 or so commandos who eventually surrendered in May 1902 were not a beaten army. They had kept at bay a force vastly superior in both numbers and equipment. Kitchener and the Boer commandants negotiated a peace settlement which, though incorporating the fallen republics within the Empire, contained important concessions in return : generous financial assistance was granted in the form of £3,000,000 to restore families to their homes and work, and interest-free loans were made available for two years; more significant was the shelving of the possible enfranchisement of non-Europeans in the Transvaal and the Free State until the two ex-republics were once more self-governing, which effectively meant that non-whites could not expect the vote.

Within five years of the peace both the Transvaal and the Free State were made self-governing colonies and had elected Afrikaner governments. The first Prime Minister of the Union of South Africa in 1910 was Louis Botha, the stalwart defender of the Tugela against Buller; he was succeeded in 1919 by another Boer general Jan Smuts, who was in turn replaced by a third ex-commando leader, J.B. Hertzog, in 1924. It hardly seemed, therefore, that the Afrikaners had lost the peace.

It is also arguable whether they lost the war. Certainly their casualties were lower, 4,000 dead as opposed to Britain's 7,000 battle deaths and 15,000 killed by disease. But it was perhaps strategically crippling to have concentrated heavily on the sieges of Ladysmith, Mafeking and Kimberley when bolder thrusts into the Cape and Natal might have shattered British morale. In any case, Roberts and Kitchener ignored the railway network obsession of the early months of the war, and turned the Boer position with sweeping and adventurous out-flanking movements. But the Afrikaners, with their limited man-power, were probably right to stick close to easily defended hill positions rather than risk a stand-up fight on the veld where their opponents would have a better chance of effectively concentrating and using the different arms of their forces. The guerilla war after Paardeberg, however, shows how outstandingly successful small forces of commandos were when deployed over huge distances.

Man for man, the short-service British recruits were far less versatile and intuitive than their civilian opponents, and their shooting rarely approached the deadly accuracy of the Boers. The Queen's troops were, however, generally courageous and steadfast in adversity, whereas the free and easy, democratic character of the commando units sometimes led to easy demoralization and dispersal when things began to go badly wrong. It is also odd that, for all their tactical success, commanders like Botha had sometimes to cajole and browbeat their men into action whereas, for all his stumblings and defeats, Buller retained the warm regard of the rank and file.

In the last resort, the British emerged from the war with one positive advantage. The tactical fiascos and deficiencies in supply and training prompted an avalanche of military reform, and many of the recommendations of a variety of commissions of enquiry were acted upon. Although these reforms did not transform the officer class into military geniuses overnight, or create subtle, hardened campaigners out of the enlisted men, they at least helped to make the British army into a better organized fighting machine when on 4 August 1914 it was pitted against an enemy far more threatening than the burghers who had ridden out from Bloemfontein and Lydenberg and Potshefstroom fifteen years before.

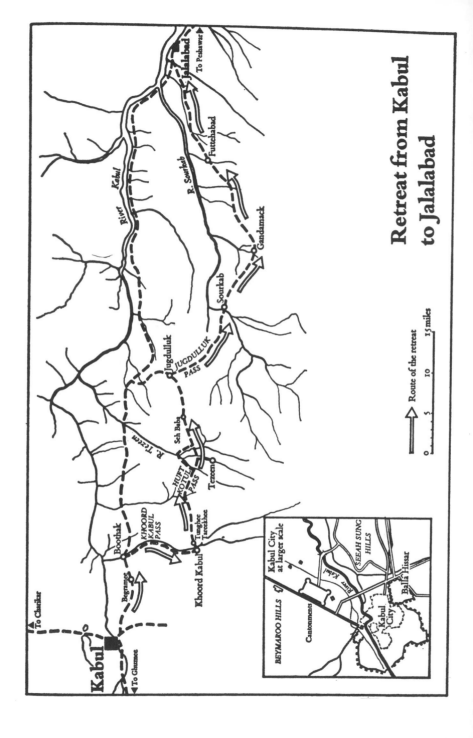

Retreat from Kabul to Jalalabad

Afghanistan and north-west India, 1838–42

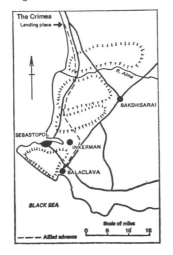

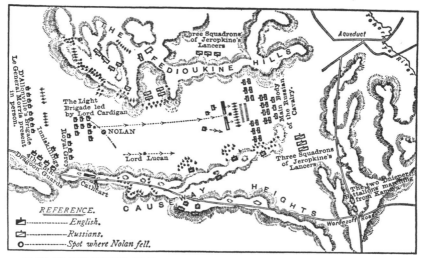

PLAN OF THE CHARGE OF THE LIGHT BRIGADE AT BALACLAVA. OCTOBER 25th, 1854

The two invasions of Zululand, 1879

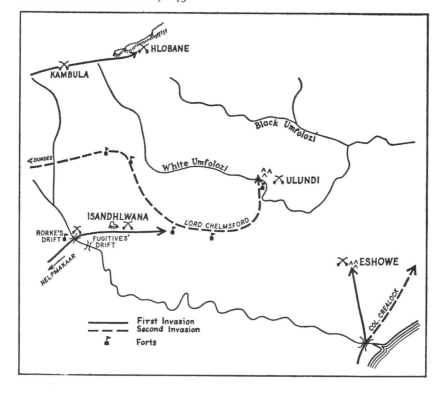

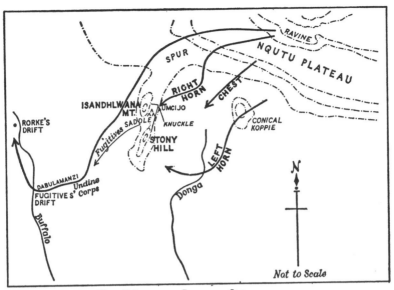

above The Battle of Isandhlwana, 22 January 1879
below Map of Colley's operations before the Battle of Majuba Hill, 1881, during the First Boer War

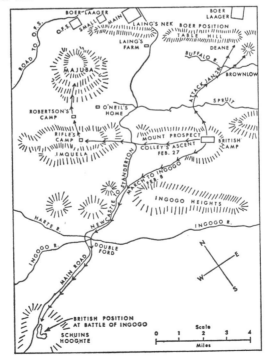

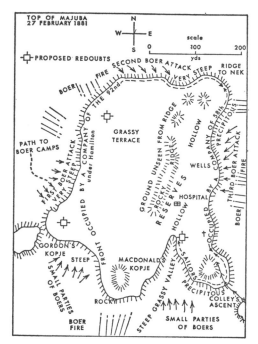

TOP OF MAJUBA
27 FEBRUARY 1881

⊕ PROPOSED REDOUBTS

BOER FIRE SECOND BOER ATTACK VERY STEEP RIDGE TO NEK

PATH TO BOER CAMPS

FIRST BOER ATTACK VERY STEEP

FRONT OCCUPIED BY A COMPANY OF THE 92nd under Hamilton

GRASSY TERRACE

GROUND UNSEEN FROM RIDGE

ROCKY RIDGE

RESERVES

HOLLOW

HOSPITAL ⊞

WELLS

OCCUPIED BY A COMPANY OF 58th

PRECIPITOUS

THIRD BOER ATTACK

BOER FIRE

GORDON'S KOPJE

STEEP

SMALL PARTIES OF BOERS

MACDONALD KOPJE

ROCKY

SAILORS HOLLOW

PRECIPITOUS

GRASSY VALLEY

COLLEY'S ASCENT

BOER FIRE

STEEP

SMALL PARTIES OF BOERS

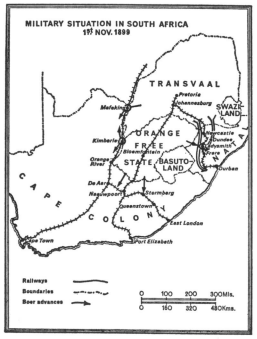

MILITARY SITUATION IN SOUTH AFRICA
1st NOV. 1899

TRANSVAAL

Mafeking

Pretoria
Johannesburg

SWAZI-LAND

ORANGE FREE STATE

Kimberley
Bloemfontein

Orange River

BASUTO-LAND

Newcastle
Dundee
Ladysmith
Frere

N A T A L

Durban

C A P E

De Aar
Naauwpoort
Stormberg
Queenstown

C O L O N Y

East London

Cape Town
Port Elizabeth

Railways ———
Boundaries —·—·—
Boer advances ——→

scale
0   100   200
yds

0   100   200   300 Mls.
0   160   320   480 Kms.

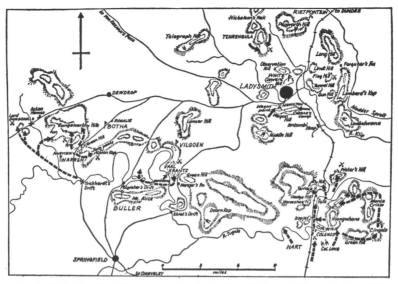

above Battlefields of the Tugela, showing Spion Kop (*left*) and Colenso (*bottom right*)
below Areas around Magersfontein and Stormberg

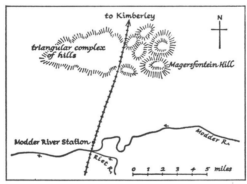

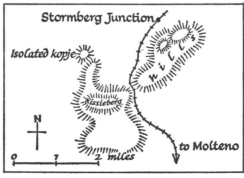

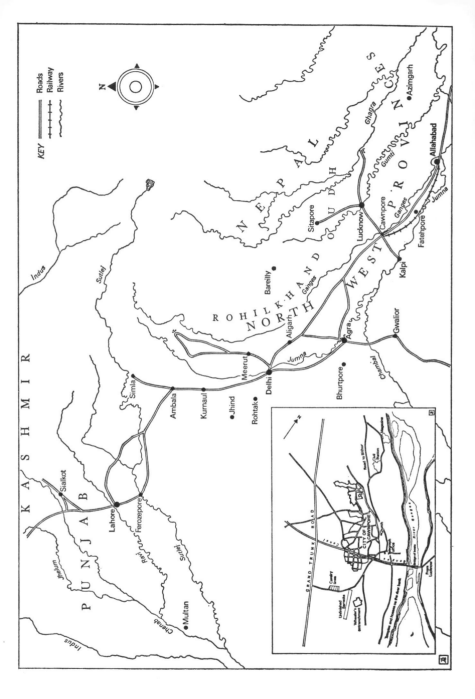

Despise not your Enemy.

A LESSON.

opposite The area most affected by the Indian Mutiny
Inset map: Plan of Cawnpore and environs

left John Bull did not, alas, fully absorb the lessons of the 1879 Zulu War

below A German cartoon mocks Britain's inability to defeat the Boers: Kitchener is portrayed as a short-sighted 'wild hunter' and the Boer as a hare, an animal which is able to conceal itself easily in natural surroundings

1901

JUGEND

Er trug die Brille auf der Nas'
Und wollte schießen todt den Has'.

Das Häschen sitzt im Blätterhaus
Und lacht den wilden Jäger aus.
(„Struwwelpeter")

Der wilde Jäger Kitchener

Appendix: Victorian Campaigns and Military Expeditions

1854–56	Crimean War
1856	Race Riots (British Guiana)
1856–57	Persian War
1856–60	Third Chinese War
1857–59	Indian Mutiny
1858	Expeditions against Tribes on North-West Frontier of India
1860–61	Second New Zealand War
1861	Sikkim Campaign
1861–62	Expeditionary Force to Canada
1863	Campaign against Tribes on North-West Frontier of India
1863–66	Third New Zealand War
1864–65	Bhootan Campaign
1865	Jamaica Rebellion
1866 and 1870	Fenian Raids (Canada)
1866–67 and 1972	Expeditions against Indians of British Honduras
1867–68	Abyssinian War
1868	Campaign against Tribes on North-West Frontier of India
1870	Red River Expedition (Canada)
1871–72	Looshai Expedition
1873–74	Ashanti War
1874	Duffla Expedition (Naga Hills)
1875–76	Perak Campaign
1875–76	Race Riots (Barbados)
1877–78	Jowakhi Campaign
1877–78	Ninth Kaffir War
1877–78	Dispatch of Indian troops to Malta (Eastern Question)
1879	Zulu War
1878–80	Second Afghan War
1880–81	First Boer War
1882	Invasion of Egypt
1884–85	Suakin Expedition

1884–85	Sudanese War
1885	Suppression of Riel's Rebellion (North-West Canada)
1885–92	The Conquest of Burma
1888	Sikkim War
1888	Hazara War (the Black Mountain Expedition)
1889–90	Chin-Looshai War
1891	Samana or Miranzai Expedition
1891	Manipur Expedition
1891	Hunza and Nagar Expedition
1892	Tambi Expedition
1892–93	Chin Hills Expedition
1893	Matabeleland Expedition
1894	Gambia Expedition
1894–95	Waziristan Expedition
1895	Defence and Relief of Chitral
1895–1900	Conquest of Ashanti
1896–99	Reconquest of the Sudan
1896	Matabeleland War
1896–97	Bechuanaland Expedition
1897	Samana or Affreedee Campaign (North-West Frontier)
1897	Benin Expedition
1897	Malakand Field Force
1899–1902	Second Boer War
1900	Fourth China War (Boxer Rebellion)

Select Bibliography

General

Anderson, D. & Killingray, D. (eds.), *Policing the Empire; Government, Authority and Control, 1850–1940* (1991)

Belich, J. *The New Zealand Wars and Victorian Interpretations of Racial Conflict* (1986)

Bolt. C., *Victorian Attitudes Towards Race* (1971)

Bond, B. (ed), *Victorian Military campaigns* (1967)

Bond, B., *The Victorian Army and the Staff College* (1972)

Chamberlain, M. E., *Pax Britannica; British Foreign Policy, 1789–1914* (1988)

Dixon, N., *On the Psychology of Military Incompetence* (1994 edition)

Eldridge, C. C., (ed.) *British Imperialism in the Nineteenth Century* (1984)

Farwell, B., *Queen Victoria's Little Wars* (1973)

Friedberg, A. *The Weary Titan; Britain and the Experience of Relative Decline* (1988)

Hobsbawm, E. J., *The Age of Empire, 1875–1914* (1994)

Johnson, F.A., *Defence by Committee* (1960)

Judd, D., *Empire; the British Imperial Experience from 1765 to the present* (1997)

Judd, D., *The Victorian Empire* (1970)

Kennedy, P., *The Rise and Fall of the Great Powers* (1987)

Knight, I. *Go to Your God Like a Soldier* (1996)

Lowe, J. C., *Britain and Foreign Affairs, 1815-85* (1998)

MacKenzie, J., *Popular Imperialism and the Military, 1850–1950* (1992)

Morris, J., *Heaven's Command* and *Pax Britannica* (vols. 1 & 2 of the *Pax Britannica* trilogy, 1979 – reissued 1999)

Hyam, R., *Britain's Imperial Century, 1815–1914* (1993 edition)

Porter, B., *The Lion's Share; a short history of British Imperialism* (1984 edition)

Robbins. K., *The Eclipse of a Great Power; Modern Britain 1870–1975* (1983)

Spears, E., *The Late-Victorian Army* (1992)

Weintraub, S., *Victoria; biography of a Queen* (1987)

The Invasion of Afghanistan

Edwardes, M., *Playing the Great Game; a Victorian Cold War* (1975)

Eyre, V., *The Military Operations at Caubul* (1843)

Fredericks, P., *The Sepoy and the Cossack* (1972)

Havelock, H., *Narrative of the War in Afghanistan* (1840)

Hough, W., *The March and Operation of the Army of the Indus* (1841)

Kaye, J.W.. *History of the War in Afghanistan* (1851)

Kaye, J. W. *Lives of the Indian Officers* (1880)

Lawrence, G., *Forty-three years in India* (1874)

Mackenzie, C., *Storms and Sunshines of a Soldier's Life* (1883)

Macrory, P., *Signal Catastrophe* (1966)

Malleson, G. B., *History of Afghanistan* (1878)

Marshman, J. C., *Memoirs of Major-General Sir Henry Havelock* (1860)

Maprayil, C., *Britain and Afghanistan; an historical perspective* (1983)

O'Ballance, E., *Afghan Wars, 1839–1992; what Britain gave up and the Soviet Union lost* (1993)

Sale, Lady, *Journal of the Disasters in Afghanistan* (1843)

Yapp, M., *Strategies of British India; Britain, Iran & Afghanistan, 1798–1850* (1980)

The Crimean War

Baumgart, W., *The Crimean War* (1999)

Brackenbury, G., *The Campaign in the Crimea* (2 vols. 1856)

Byrne, M., *Britain and the European Powers 1815–65* (1998)

Douglas, G., *The Devil's Own* (1997)

Douglas, G., *The Valley of Death* (1998)

French Blake, R. L. V., *The Crimean War* (1992)

Goldfrank, D. M., *The Origins of the Crimean War* (1993)

Duberly, H. *Journal Kept during the Russian War* (1855)

Gibbs, P. *Crimean Blunder* (1960)
Hibbert, C. *The Destruction of Lord Raglan* (1961)
Kerr, P., *The Crimean War* (1997)
Kingslake, A. W., *The Invasion of the Crimea* (8 vols. 1887)
Judd, D., *The Crimean War* (1977)
Palmer, A. *The Crimean War* (1992)
Russell, W. H., *The British Expedition to the Crimea* (1858)
Selby, J. M., *The Thin Red Line* (1970)
Warner, P. (ed.), *Letters Home from the Crimea* (1999)
Williamson, L., *Florence Nightingale and the Birth of Professional Nursing* (1999)
Woodham-Smith, C., *The Reason Why* (1953)

The Indian Mutiny

Bartrum, K., *A Widow's Reminiscences of Lucknow* (1858)
Germon, M. *Journal of the Siege of Lucknow* (1958)
Gimlette, G. *A Postscript to the Records of the Indian Mutiny* (1927)
Heathcote, T. A., *The Military in British India; the development of British land forces in South Asia, 1600–1947* (1994)
Hewitt, J. (ed.), *Eye Witnesses to the Indian Mutiny* (1972)
Hibbert, C. *The Great Mutiny; India 1857* (1980)
Kaye, J. W., *History of the Sepoy War* (3 vols. 1880)
Majendie, Lieutenant, *Up Among the Pandies* (1859)
Mason, P., *A Matter of Honour; an account of the Indian Army, its officers and men* (1974)
Lunt, J. (ed.), *From Sepoy to Subedar; being the life and adventures of Subedar Sita Ram, a native officer in the Bengal Army* (1998 edition)
Palmer, J. A. B., *The Mutiny Outbreak at Meerut* (1966)
Pemble, J., *The Raj, the Indian Mutiny and the Kingdom of Oudh, 1801–1859* (1977)
Roberts, Lord, *Fifty-one Years in India* (1898)
Robinson, J., *Angels of Albion; Women of the Indian Mutiny* (1996)
Russell, W. H., *My Indian Mutiny Diary* (1957)
Sen, S. N., *Eighteen Fifty Seven* (1957)
Stokes, E. (ed. Bayly, C. A.), *The Peasant Armed; the Indian Rebellion of 1857* (1986)

Ward, A., *Our Bones Are Scattered; the Cawnpore Massacres and the Indian Mutiny of 1857* (1996)

Wood, E., *The Revolt in Hindoostan, 1857–59* (1908)

The Zulu War

Ashe, Major & Wyatt-Edgell, E. V., *The Story of the Zulu Campaign* (1880)

Clammer, D., *The Zulu War* (1973)

Edgerton, R. B., *Like Lions They Fought; the Zulu War and the Last Black Empire in South Africa* (1988)

French, G., *Lord Chelmsford and the Zulu War* (1939)

Furneaux, R., *The Zulu War; Isandhlwana and Rorke's Drift* (1963)

Guy, J., *The Destruction of the Zulu Kingdom; the Civil War in Zululand, 1879-84* (1979)

Hallam-Parr, H., *A Sketch of the Kafir and Zulu Wars* (1880)

Knight, I., *The Anatomy of the Zulu Army* (1999)

Laband, J., *Kingdom in Crisis; the Zulu response to the Invasion of 1879* (1992)

Morris, D. R., *The Washing of the Spears* (1966)

Morris-Newman, C. L., *In Zululand with the British Throughout the War of 1879* (1880)

Smith-Dorrien, H., *Memories of Forty Eight Years' Service* (1925)

Wood, E., *From Midshipman to Field Marshal* (1906)

The First Boer War, 1880–81

Bellairs, B. St.J., *The Transvaal War 1880–1* (1885)

Butler, W. F., *Life of Sir George Pomeroy-Colley* (1899)

Carter, T. F., *A Narrative of the Boer War* (1896)

Cromb. J., *The Majuba Disaster* (1891)

De Kieweit, C. W. *The Imperial Factor in South Africa* (1976)

Fisher, W. E. G., *The Transvaal and the Boers* (1896)

Haggard, R., *The Last Boer War* (1899)

Harrison, D., *The White Tribe of Africa* (1981)

Kruger, P. *The Memoirs of Paul Kruger* (1902)

Lehmann, J., *The First Boer War* (1972)

Nixon, J., *The Complete Story of the Transvaal* (1885)

Norris-Newman, C. L., *With the Boers in the Transvaal and the Orange Free State 1880–1* (1882)

Ransford, O., *The Battle of Majuba Hill* (1967)

Uys, C. J., *In the Era of Shepstone* (1933)

Wilson, M. & Thompson, L., *The Oxford History of South Africa* (1975)

The Second Boer War, 1899–1902

Amery, L. S. (Ed.), *Times History of the War in South Africa* (vols. 1–7, 1900–09)

Comaroff, J. L. (Ed.), *The Boer War Diary of Sol. T. Plaatje; an African at Mafeking* (1973)

Conan Doyle, A., *The Great Boer War* (1902)

De Wet, C., *Three Years' War* (1903)

Farwell, B., *The Great Boer War* (1977 edition)

Fisher, J., *That Miss Hobhouse* (1971)

Gardner, B., *Mafeking; a Victorian Legend* (1966)

Gardner, B., *The Lion Caged; Cecil Rhodes and the Siege of Kimberley* (1969)

Jeal, T., *Baden-Powell* (1989)

Judd, D., *The Boer War* (1977)

Kammack, D., *The Rand at War* (1991)

Marais, J. S., *The Fall of Kruger's Republic* (1961)

Meintjes, J., *President Paul Kruger* (1974)

Meintjes, J., *General Louis Botha* (1970)

Nasson, B., *The South African War, 1899–1902* (1999)

Pakenham, T., *The Boer War* (1979)

Pemberton, W. B. *Battles of the Boer War* (1964)

Price, R. *An Imperial War and the British Working class; working class attitudes and reaction to the Boer War* (1972)

Ransford, O., *The Battle of Spion Kop* (1969)

Reitz, D., *Commando* (1929)

Sandys, C. *Churchill Wanted Dead or Alive* (1999)

Stirling, J., *Our Regiments in South Africa* (1903)

Surridge, K., *Managing the South African War, 1899–1902; Politicians versus the Generals.* (1999)

Thomas, A., *Rhodes; the race for Africa* (1996)

Wilson, H. W., *With the Flag to Pretoria* (vols. 1 & 2, 1901)

Index

GREAT BATTLES SERIES

HASTINGS
Peter Poyntz Wright
Paperback £9.99 Illustrated

AGINCOURT
Christopher Hibbert
Paperback £9.99 Illustrated

THE BATTLE OF THE BOYNE AND AUGHRIM:
THE WAR OF THE TWO KINGS
John Kinross
Paperback £10.99 Illustrated

CORUNNA
Christopher Hibbert
Paperback £12.99 Illustrated

WELLINGTON'S PENINSULAR VICTORIES
Michael Glover
Paperback £12.99 Illustrated

TRAFALGAR: THE NELSON TOUCH
David Howarth
Paperback £10.99 Illustrated

BORODINO
Digby Smith
Paperback £12.99 Illustrated

WATERLOO: A NEAR RUN THING
David Howarth
Paperback £12.99 Illustrated

ARNHEM
Christopher Hibbert
Paperback £10.99 Illustrated

Order from THE WINDRUSH PRESS, LITTLE WINDOW, HIGH
STREET, MORETON-IN-MARSH, GLOS. GL56 0LL
MAJOR CREDIT CARDS ACCEPTED
TEL: 01608 652012 FAX: 01608 652125
Please add £1 post and packing within the UK